íf

you're a wee bít írísh

A CHART OF OLD

IRISH FAMILIES

collected from folk tradition

Library of Congress Catalogue Number 78-61121

International Standard Book Number 0-9601868-0-8

Printed in the United States of America

Original Printing December 31, 1978

Second Printing, November, 1979

Third Printing, February, 1981

Production
Irv's Print Shop
San Diego, California

Published by

The Irish Family Names Society
P.O. Box 2095
La Mesa, California, 92041

IF YOU'RE A WEE BIT IRISH

By

Ulliam O'Duirnin

A guide to family relationships
as collected from the oral tradition

Dedicated To:

Billy Durning
Poet-Farmer
and
Head of the Clan in Ireland

and

Clifton Hunter, Historian
of
Gunter, Texas

and to

Everyone, who feels

"A Wee Bit Irish"

The encouragement of dedicated friends
made years of search worth the effort.

Cover By:
Clayton Clark, III

Art
Suzanne
Fitzpatrick

INTRODUCTION

Oral tradition has long been recognized as a valuable source of Irish Family history.

A recent trend in ancestral research has heightened the interest in our ancestry prior to documented history, and provided the encouragement needed to seek out our oldest relatives and a retelling of old family traditions. Interviews over a number of years with these older generations in Ireland, England and America are the basis of the tables to follow.

We choose to call "If You're A Wee Bit Irish" an "Index to Families" rather than a Genealogy, (assuming a genealogy to be based on documented fact), because these charts have been assembled from folk memory and do not in every case follow the documented pattern. We believe this is a valid approach since many families have left little or no trace in public records. Surviving folk tradition then is the only source from which information regarding such families can be obtained. The function of the Society then, is to collect from folk tradition, record, publish, and purify as time permits.

Someone has said, "Every Irishman has a King or a Queen for an ancestor". The charts to follow seem to carry out this tradition. Many important persons have been shown in CAPITAL LETTERS for easy identification.

More than 800 family names appear in the Index which, together with Irish and English variations, number more than 2000. The lineage of most of these families shows gaps yet to be filled in. "Gap Filling" is a continuing project of the Society. This particular volume deals with family relationships from earliest times down to 1600. Persons with surnames forming at a later date and immigrants to Ireland after 1600 will be the subject of a later work. Meanwhile it is believed that this is the most complete chart of family relationships available from oral sources.

It is our hope that this little book will be a valuable aid in your own personal search.

The Irish Family Names Society

TABLE OF CONTENTS

Poems by; Billy Durning, County Donegal, Ireland

This book is published directly from the authors
manuscript to speed it's release date.

THE SHEPHERD'S MORNING WALK

The first faint glow of early dawn
Was stealing o'er the hilltops brown
When to the mountains with his dogs
The shepherd trods the mirey bogs
Naught else to greet the morning beam
But whispering winds and bubbling streams

All nature's creatures still at rest
Per chance meandering dogs molest
The frightened hares spring up and go
The startled moorcocks loudly crow
Sharp echoes through the lonely glen
Then all is silent once again

The gathering light his pathway shows
And higher up the hill he goes
Until he gains a vantage sight
As dawning day replaces night
Commands his dogs to round the sheep
And views them on the hillside steep

His work now done he scans the scene
The clustered hills and glens between
His homeward path he does retrace
From summit high to lowly base
Enjoying now the wild bird's song
As he greets the morning's cheery dawn

THE SEARCH

Once I had decided to "look up" my ancestors, I considered the task a simple one. A quick visit to the library, a few hours spent, and the task would be done - that was 30 years ago, and I am still searching.

I did learn that my family name first occurred in historical records about 1225 and that in the following 753 years the activities of all our generations filled less than one printed page. All was not lost, however, for when other methods failed I decided to ferret out folk history in the present generation by writing hundreds of letters, visiting Europe and interviewing people. I uncovered very little information about my own family but much about others and how we all fit together - Irish Style, and that is what is to be found in this book.

While much has been written about Irish families, great gaps exist in our heritage and folklore appears to be the only way to fill the void.

Oral family history fell into disfavor with the coming of the scientific era. But the merit of stories told by our ancestors can be found in facts, perhaps distorted, but still one good source from which factual history can be partially restored. The charts which follow have been compiled from oral tradition. I do not wish to present them as genealogy (which I define as identifying specific individuals by documented facts collected from historical sources), but rather as folk tradition collected from oral sources which parallels in many respects the old Irish genealogies.

Numerous informants recalled tales from their childhood extending into a still more distant past. Whatever the truth may be, folklore has made possible a much more interesting "History" for many of us than could be gleaned from public records.

From the genealogist's point of view, it is much less difficult to "correct" than to "collect". In this book I have concentrated on "collection" since with the present generation this opportunity may pass; and I shall leave "correction" for a later date.

Ulliam O'Duirnin

THE PARTING

Farewell, farewell, a last farewell; the parting
  time has come.
The bus that serves the train and boat, I hear
  its distant hum.
One last embrace, one last fond look, in melting
  tears we part,
With sob and sigh and heart pang sore, we feel
  the stinging dart.

Then from their humble homes they go, a livelihood
  to seek.
The arrows in their hearts they show, as tears
  roll down their cheeks.
A lonesome backward glance they take, ere friends
  fade out of view,
And to their home and family all, they wave a
  fond adieu.

Their voice in song no more we hear, nor laughter
  blithe and gay;
No more their voice in prayer so dear, at family
  Rosary.
When seated by the hearth fire bright when winter
  nights are o'er,
We think of former pastimes gay, of mirth and joy
  and cheer.

THE BEGINNING

Irish ancient history can be confusing because of the similarity of names of persons who lived in different time periods. It is for those who wish to have a better understanding of how family names fit into Irish history that this book will be especially valuable.

The charts begin with Adam, as was the custom among the early Christian Irish, and many other Europeans. It traces the beginning of the nations in the Biblical manner, eventually narrowing down to the Gaelic Irish and terminating with the beginning of the English surnames. This means that most portions of the charts end around 1600. From this time on most of our family names can be traced in conventional documents.

The Author is preparing an Irish folk history with its characters keyed to the charts in this book. However, this project is a year or more away from completion. In the meantime a checklist of helpful reference works has been provided which can be consulted for details of many persons who appear in the charts.

We are all interested in our family name, of course, and over 800 of the older Irish families are mentioned in this book. Some of my informants provided detailed ancestral information. Still others had sketchy knowledge, connecting themselves only to some remote ancestor of historical note.

The charts do not extend to the more recent inhabitants of Ireland, such as the Scotts-Irish, Huguenots, New English, Germans or Spanish. The roots of these relative newcomers (arrival after 1500) should properly begin with histories in other countries. Tracing these lines must await some future date. Many prominent old Irish families are also missing. This is due to their not being directly connected with the original objective of my ancestral search. To these families I offer my apology.

Ancient Irish historians considered the Scythians (page 11) to be their remote ancestors. Herodotus, in his "Histories" has given us a vivid picture of these people and their nomadic life. A close

parallel appears to exist between his description
of them and the Gaelic Irish of the same period.
Irish tales tell the story of Niul (page 11), who
lived in Egypt and married a princess of that country. It was fashionable during the 1800's to consider this a farfetched tale. However, we now know
that Ireland was not out of reach of Egyptian ship-
ping of the period, and that peasant clothing of
the old Gaelic Irish more closely resembled Egyptian
than that of the Scythians.

Two diverse societies have long existed in Europe.
The first I call The Settled People, comprising
those who lived in one place for a long period and
who were primarily concerned with food and protec-
tion.

In opposition to the settled people were the
Nomadics. Their principal need was pasture land and
food, and they traveled as the seasons changed,
following their cattle which were both their wealth
and food.

The ancient Irish further divided these two civilizations into three distinct social structures:

The Low Land Settled Peoples:

Mostly dark skinned, dark eyed, short, and curly
haired they were inhabitants of the lands around
the Mediterranean. Quick witted, alert, ingenious,
clever, ambitious and inventive, they could visu-
alize and manage. Prolific builders, they con-
structed great stone works all over western Europe
and were the "Engineers" of later Greek and Roman
societies. Relatives in Africa were responsible
for the great public works there. These were the
people who laid the foundations of the sciences
which made the trip to the moon possible in our
generation.

High Land Settled Peoples:

These ancestors of ours were sturdily built. They
could perform feats of strength which left the Mediterranean lowlanders shaking their heads. They were
of medium stature, light to dark eyes, broad chested
with straight dark brown to black hair. Their prime

characteristic was reliability. They could be shown
a task and would pursue it for hours on end, attend-
ing to the minutest details without tiring. They
made stone axes by the millions. These axes, which
appear useless to us, felled the forests of Europe
and made agriculture possible. These highlanders
were reliable slaves and were probably traded to the
Mediterraneans by their northern neighbors, the
Nomads. Their genetic descendants are the techni-
cians of today.

The Nomads of the North:

The Nomads could best be characterized as the people
possessing an aggressive independence. They were a
tall, light haired people, although by the time of
Herodotus they were thoroughly mixed with their
neighbors and came in a variety of shapes, sizes and
colors. Among the Scythians at least the common
denominator was language. In fact the possession
of language was their greatest art. Language plus
an astonishingly well trained memory made it possible to create an amazingly complex civilization
without the need to reduce any part of it to writing.
Their laws were oral and they were past masters of
music and song. They had little difficulty learning
the languages of others, and as a result were the
go-betweens and traders for the nations surrounding
them. They were extremely athletic and one even
suspects that the statues of early Greek athletic
heroes may, in fact, really represent Scythians per-
forming under contract to the Greeks. In later
times they were the driving wedge of most European
armies, for they were superb soldiers and horsemen.

The civilizations of the settled and nomadic peoples
were in opposition. The Nomad, depending on memory
and oral transmission of important facts, embel-
lished every story as an aid to memory. The lis-
tener, in turn, had the unique ability of stripping
away the embellishment and retaining the essen-
tials. In later times many of the old tales were
written by scribes from the "Fixed People" just as
told and, therefore, give us a very queer impression
of the Nomad. Most of us today have been trained
in the settled rather than the nomadic culture,
and do not have a full appreciation of this branch

of our ancestry.

One characteristic of the "fixed" life was of considerable importance. We call it the ability to
duplicate, or mass production. This ability was
present in the yearly planting of crops, building
of buildings and the making of tools.

The weak spot in the "Nomadic" structure was con-
tinuity. Disrupt a generation or two and the whole
social structure could fall or at best become
greatly distorted.

Unlike person-to-person transmission of ideas, writing, when scribed on permanent material, could pass
easily from generation to generation. Since this
tool of the fixed society was precise and logical,
historians in later generations could reconstruct
an old written language even though it might have
fallen from use centuries before.

Thus, most stories of contact with the nomadics are
written reports by a member of the fixed society,
giving a one-sided view of these people. Almost
always the Nomad is pictured as an aggressor simply
because in his travels he had crossed the lands
of the fixed people and he was war like. When he
served in the armies of the Greeks, Romans and
others, and gave them victories the fixed society,
of course, took the credit. Numerous examples
could be cited.

Fortunately, archaeology is giving us a better understanding of our nomadic ancestors. A closer look
is also being given to their tales written around
the beginning of the Christian era. Slowly a new
and more correct view of our inheritance is emerg-
ing.

Of course we have become so thoroughly mixed in
today's society that we no longer retain the simple
genetic qualities of our ancestors, but rather we
are a mixed bag with family members exhibiting
features of all our past ancestry in varying degrees.

Those of us who are a "Wee Bit Irish" are the most
polyglot mixture of all these marvelous ancestral
peoples. What makes us "Irish" is a feeling of

closeness to the mother land transmitted by the
genes of a not-too-remote native Irish person.
And, of course, one who visits Ireland is "Irish"
forever.

The record of our ancestors which follows will perhaps contribute to this new search of our past,
and give us each a clearer understanding of our-
selves.

My fond hope, which I believe is possible, is to one
day create an accurate table of relationships for
most Irish families. For such a wee island, and
such a great people, is this too much ambition? No,
I think not.

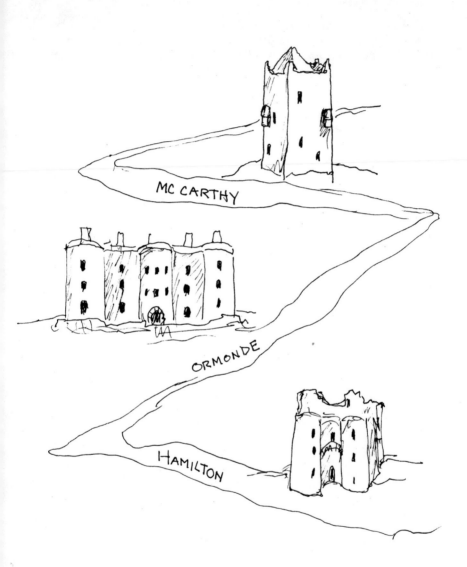

MC CARTHY

ORMONDE

HAMILTON

OUR FAMILY HEROES IN FOLK TRADITION

We Irish are a fortunate lot for it is rather easy
to find Kings, Queens and heroes among our ancestors. The charts make locating them a simple
matter. Many persons of special interest are
shown in capital letters. Each time your family
line passes through a CAPITALIZED name, that person
can usually be found in an Irish history book.

To provide a quick look into your past I have selected the following examples of such persons.
Those from pre-history have been listed first. Following these are the four divisions of the Gaelic
Irish and finally representative persons among the
later invaders.

Start your search by tracing over the connecting
lines from your name to the front of the book. When
it passes through one of the persons in the following list stop for a moment and read up on your very
own "Family Hero"!

ADAM   Page 1
Considered by the Irish of the Christian Era (and
some think at an earlier date), to be their earliest
ancestor.

BRIOTAN MAOL   Page 5
Ancestor of the welsh clans and of Saint Patrick.

CAIBRE CINN CAIT   Page 6   50 AD
A slave of the old race who became the rebel king
of Ireland.

EOCHAIDH OLLATHAR   Page 7   1400 BC
Called "The Daga Mor", and classified by some historians as a god of the Tuatha de Danann. He is
also said to have been the king of the Tuatha de
Danann before the Milesians arrived.

THE FIRBOLG   Page 5   1560 BC
An ancient farming and fishing people who, escaping
from slavery in Greece, made their way to Ireland.

THE FOMORIANS   Pages 7 & 10
A pirate race assumed to have come from Phoenician colonies in North Africa. Later they moved to Scandinavia and on occasion took up residence on Tory Island, off the northwest coast of Ireland, and from there raided the mainland.

GOMER   Page 3   2250 BC
Brother of Magog and son of Japheth. He is considered to be the ancestor of one of the main branches of the tribes that populated Europe.

IARBHOINEOL FAIDH   Page 5   1700 BC
He was in the kingly line of the Scythians who, in their wanderings, lived in Greece and Africa.

JAPHETH   Page 1
Son of Noah and ancestor of the Scythians, who, in turn, became the ancestors of the Celts, according to legend.

LUIGHAIDH LAMBHFADH   Page 10   1420 BC
Called "The Long Armed One", he was the foster son of TAILLTE. He is said to have been the first to hold an assembly in honor of a foster parent. The event became an annual gathering and eventually the "Olympics" of Ireland became a part of it. In later centuries, parents added "match making", finding this an ideal opportunity to select brides for their sons.

MAGOG   Page 3
Son of Japheth and, according to tradition, ancestor of the Celts and thus the Irish.

MAOIN   Page 6   150 AD
"Wearer of the Golden Collar". Believed to represent the sun god. He was a maker of just laws. He is said to have refused the kingship of Ireland because he was not of Milesian ancestry.

NEMEDIUS   Page 5   1740 BC
Ancestor of a branch of the Scythian-Greeks called the Firbolg (or "Men of the Leather Bags"). Some say he was the progenitor of the Tuatha de Danann also.

NIUL   Page 11   1585 BC
Son of King Feinius Farsadh of Scythia. He was a
master of the tribal languages of Europe. Egypt,
a trading nation, asked that this son be sent to
them to organize a language school. The Pharaohos
of this period were probably Hyksos. The monarch,
perhaps a distant relative of the Scythian King,
gave his daughter, Scota, in marriage to Niul.
According to tradition it is from this pair that the
Gaelic Irish are derived.

NUADHA   Page 7   1467 BC
"The Silver Hand". A king of the Tuatha de Danann
who lost his hand in battle (thus disqualifying him
to be king). His silversmith, however, made him a
fully functional one of silver.

PARTHOLON   Page 4
First of the Scythian Greeks to bring his clan to
Ireland.

CORMAC CAS   Pages 17 & 23   250 AD
Son of Oilill Olom, "The Wise", and ancestor of the
collective family called The Dal Cais.

CONAL CLAINGHEACH   Page 37   120 BC
A King whose life was saved by his chief poet who
thoughtfully seated him among the poets rather than
his usual place. His enemies being more afraid of
the poets than the king, did not harm him.

CONOR MAC NESSA   Page 37   1 AD
Said to have been born about the time of Christ, he
is said to have had a revelation of Christ's birth.

CORMAC CONNLONGES   Page 37   30 AD
Went into exile because hostages in his keeping had
been killed.

CU-CHULAINN (Setanta) Page 37
One of old Ireland's greatest heroes. His mother
was Irish but his father was said to have been a
foreigner. He was short and dark complected. At
the age of 7 he became a soldier in King Cormac's
army. He died in battle at age 27.

EOCHAIDH OLLAM FODHLA   Page 35   924 BC
The first high king of Ireland to organize a genealogical and political convention.

FEARGHUS MAC ROICH   Page 41
King of Ulster. Tricked into resigning the kingship
by the beautiful Nessa.

SAINT MALACHY   Page 40
He built the church at Bangor of stone rather than
wood making this building material popular in Ireland.

MACHA MONGRUADH   Pages 36 & 41   377 BC
Called "The Golden Head" she was the 76th monarch
of Ireland. She personally supervised the building
of her palace at Emain Macha. She was the daughter
of the great Aed Ruadh (Hugh Roe).

NESSA   Page 37   25 BC
Until the church forbade it, women went into battle
with their men. Nessa was a warrior queen.

HEREMON (Eremon)   Page 12   1034 BC
A son of Mile and ancestor of one of the four
branches of the Gaelic Irish. The Picts arrived
during his reign as king. He gave them wives and
sent them to Scotland with the understanding that
the line of the reigning monarch would descend
through the female (and thus be Irish) rather than
the male line.

CRIOMTHANN (Crimthann)   Page 17   240 AD
Brother of Mong Fionn (Pages 17 and 53) whom she
made king. In later years she poisoned him but to
do so had to take poison herself.

EOCHAIDH BAILLDEARG   Page 24   470 AD
Nicknamed "The Red Mole" he was an ancestor of the
famous king Brian Boroimhe, and was baptized by
Saint Patrick

FINN MAC COOL
(Fionn Mac Cumail)   Page 23   250 AD
A hero of Scotland as well as Ireland. He was a
leader of the FIANNA, a military band who enforced
the king's orders but also spent a great deal of
time having fun. Finn was the husband of Albe,
the daughter of Cormac Ulfhada (Page 52).

OILILL OLOM   Page 17   200 AD
Remembered for his faithful adherence to the law and
for skillfully uniting opposing families through
marriage.

HEBER FIONN
(Eber Finn)   Page 12   1045 BC
A son of Mile, also the prime ancestor of one line
of the Gaelic Irish. Heber's wife coveted part of
the land assigned to his brother Heremon, resulting
in the first war between these brothers.

EOGAN MOR   Page 17   220 AD
Although some of the Irish may have been Christian
at this time, Eogan continued worship of the old
god Nodon (Nuadu?), introduced into Ireland by the
Tuatha de Danann.

IR   Page 12   145 BC
Another son of Mile, one of the four original ancestors of the Gaelic Irish.

AILILL   Page 41
Father of the Seven Maines and husband of Queen
Maeve (Page 49) of Connacht (Maeve had other
husbands previously from the north of Ireland).
A joking comparison of the wealth of each (for
women held property in their own right in ancient
Ireland) ended in a war with the north called
"The Great Cattle Raid of Cooley" (Cuailgne).

SAINT CIARAN   Page 41   520 AD
Founder of the monastery of Clonmacnois. This in-
stitution (now in ruins) became an international
university and was said to have had as many as 5000
students before the coming of the Normans. Legend
also says that in the late 1300's a space ship
appeared overhead and was seen by everyone who had
come for Sunday Mass.

ART AONFHIR   Page 50   185 AD
"The Lonely One". Son of the famous Conn of the
Hundred Battles, he was also the father of Cormac
Art. Some say that in his travels he became ac-
quainted with Christianity and had a vision of its
spread all over Ireland.

XX

SAINT BRIGHID (Bride)   Page 50   475 AD
One of Ireland's great Christian leaders. She
dearly loved animals and was noted far and wide for
her generosity. She founded a religious house in
Kildare.

CAIBRE RIADA   Page 48   490 AD
He led a migration of his followers from Kerry to
Antrim. Many of them later crossed over to Scot-
land.

THE COLLAS   Page 65   315 AD
They were the ancestors of one clan of Irish mercenary soldiers. In later times they were a mixture
of Irish, Scotch and Norse, called "The Galloglas".

SAINT COLUMBIA   Page 86   455 AD
An emotional churchman and poet. His copying a book
caused a war between churchmen and for this sin he
banished himself to the Island of Iona off the west
coast of Scotland.

RODERICK O'CONOR
(Ruadhe O'Conchubhair) Pages 59 & 62
High King of Ireland when the Normans came. He
appears to have been a brilliant, well educated man
but, unfortunately, his military ability could not
match that of his father. He has been blamed, perhaps unjustly, for the Norman invasion of Ireland.

DATHY   Page 70   398 AD
This man has been credited with numerous raids upon
the European continent. He died near the Alps and
his comrades returned his body to Ireland, burying
him near where the king's palace stood in the Province of Connacht. People living in that community
today point out a standing stone which they say
marks his grave.

DEARBFORGAIL (Dervilia) Page 56   1170 AD
Wife of O'Ruairc. The old histories say she had an
affair with or was purloined away by King Mac Murrough, thus beginning a chain of events which some
say brought on the Norman invasion of Ireland.

DIARMUID and GRAINNE   Page 52   250 AD
Two great lovers in the oldest Irish tradition.
They were pursued all over Ireland by a jealous
king, at last dying in each others arms.

EVA   Page 94   1180 AD
Pawn in the O'Ruarc-Mac Murrough-Norman invasion
affair. She was promised by King Mac Morrow to the
Norman Earl, Strongbow, for his aid in the invasion
of Ireland (which in Norman Law would give him
title to Mac Morrough's lands in Ireland). Many
poems have been written about her sacrifice.

DIARMUID MAC MORROUGH   Page 94   1170 AD
Father of Eva (above), it was through his invitation
that the Normans came to Ireland.

DULACH GALACH   Page 53   425 AD
Grandson of EOCHAIDH MOIDHMEODHAIN and ancestor of
the O'Conors and their various branches.

EARC   Page 48   503 AD
Father of Fergus who went to Scotland as the Chief
of the Irish Dial Riada.

EOCHAIDH AIREAMH   Page 49   75 BC
Introduced burial in graves as a substitute for cre-
mation.

EOCHAIDH FIEDLIOC   Page 49   75 BC
King of Ireland and builder of the palace at Rath
Crogan in the Province of Connacht. He was the
father of Queen Maeve and the three Fineniana. The
O'Conors were descended from this king and connected
with Rath Crogan in historical times. Nothing remains of the old buildings.

FIACAD FIONOUD   Page 49
Owner of "The White Cows", apparently something to
be proud of (most cattle were black). He was the
founder of the great family group called the "Dial
Fiatach".

GRACE O'MALLEY   Page 53   1600 AD
Queen Elizabeth was said to have appreciated her
ability as a sea captain and pirate.

GUIRE   Page 71
"The Hospitable". Considered one of the most gener-
ous of the old Irish Chieftains, especially with
poets. He may have had a part in the plot to kill
Saint Cellach, although the chart shows approxi-
mately 80 years between them.

MUIRCHEARTACH   Pages 78 & 103   443 AD
"Inventor of the Leather Cloaks". Today we would
call him the inventor of the furlined sleeping
bag, which made it possible for him to wage war in
winter. The O'Neills of Ulster are his descendants.

MUIREADHACH MUILLEATHAN   Page 54   700 AD
From him came the Siol Muiredhaigh (The Seed of
Murry), a collective name for the clans to which
the O'Conors belonged.

OILILL MOLT   Page 70   470 AD
Ancestor of the warrior chief Eogan Bel (who had
himself buried standing up facing his enemies), and
the precedent of Saint Cellach, a student at Cluinmacnois.

CONN BACHACH O'NEILL   Page 80   1550 AD
One of the last provincial kings to "go over" to
the English. He gave up his Gaelic title of "The
O'Neill" to become The Earl of Tyrone.

NIALL NAOIGHIALLACH   Page 52   400 AD
"Of the Nine Hostages". Foster son of the great
Ollam Torna (Chief Poet) whose influence made Niall
one of the great High Kings of Ireland.

TIGHEARNMHAS   Page 44   900 BC
During his reign Ireland appears to have engaged in
a brisk overseas trade. Among other items he im-
ported dyes blue, green and saffron.

SAINT LAWRENCE O'TOOLE   Page 93   1170 AD
Mediator between the Irish and the English during
the reign of Roderick O'Conor.

CORMAC ULFHADA   Page 52   253 AD
Built a building large enough to shelter 1000 persons. Some say that as of this date it was the
largest structure in northern Europe.

OUTSIDERS WHO ARRIVED IN IRELAND
AFTER THE GAELS

SAINT PATRICK   Page 7   450 AD
His family was Christian and probably of the old
Welsh-Saxon stock. They appear to have been well
treated by the Romans. Patrick was captured by an
Irish raiding party and carried back to the north
of Ireland. He was a slave for an Irish Chief and
given the job of sheep herder. Some years later he
escaped and made his way to Europe where he became
a priest. He felt the call of the Spirit and returned to the Irish people as a missionary. Although there were missionaries to the Irish both
before and after his time, there is no doubt that
his example of hardship and persistence was un-
matched.

GORM ESKE   Page 100   900 AD
Called "The English Man", King of Denmark.

HAROLD BLUE TOOTH   Page 101   930 AD
First Christian King of Denmark.

HAROLD FAIRHAIR   Page 100   890 AD
King of Norway.

LEIF ERICKSON   Page 104   870 AD
Born in the Viking colony in Greenland.

MANGUS BARELEGS   Page 101   1130 AD
King of Norway who changed custom by wearing typical
Irish trousers which came to the knee only.

ODIN (Woden)   Page 99   1150 BC
A hero who brought his people across Europe from
the site of Troy to present day Denmark. Folk tradition made him a god of the Norse and German
peoples.

OLAF CURRAN   Page 102   894 AD
Called "Olaf the Red", King of Denmark.

RENAR LODBROG   Page 99   810 AD
Probably the same as the Viking invader of Ireland
called Turgesius.

ROLLO (Rolf)   Page 105   890 AD
A famous Viking leader who established the Kingdom
of Normandy, and was the ancestor of William the
Conqueror.

SNORI   Page 104   900 AD
First of the Vikings to be born in North America.
He became one of the great oral historians.

EARL STRONGBOW   Pages 108 & 114   1140 AD
The popular nickname of Earl Richard de Clare of
Pembroke in Wales. A conqueror of Ireland, who
married Eva Mac Morrough as part of the agreement
for his invading.

GERALDUS CAMBRENSIS   Page 108   1150 AD
A Norman-Welsh historian who wrote about the ex-
periences of the Normans in Ireland.

HENRY I   Pages 106 & 111   1130 AD
King of England. He and the famous Welsh lady,
Nesta, are the ancestors of one branch of the Invaders of Ireland. Nesta had children by other
husbands who were also part of the expedition.

NESTA I   Pages 106,107,108,111   1135 AD
Considered to be one of the most beautiful ladies
in Wales. She was called "The Mother of the Irish
Invasion" because of her role as mother and sister
of several of the invasion leaders.

RAYMOND le GROS   Page 109   1188 AD
"The Fat One". One of the most aggressive invaders.

The MAC FIRBIS Family   Page 70
Historians and one of the families responsible for
the old genealogies which have been preserved.
Duald Mac Firbis lived about 1650 and wrote his
"Great Book of Genealogies" during the Cromwellian
War.

"TRIM CASTLE" County - Meath

HOW TO USE THE CHARTS

FIRST:

Locate your family name in the index. Read "Our Family Names" (Page 116) for further details.

NEXT:

Turn to the chart page number where your surname appears.

FIND YOUR TRADITIONAL ANCESTRY:

Beginning at your surname, trace over the connecting lines from that point to the front of the book. Use a transparent coloring pen. Numbers in parentheses locate at least one County of residence where persons of your family name lived.

As you progress some names will be in capital letters. Many of these persons have a place in recorded history and a small selected group will be found in this book beginning on Page XV.

Children in the tables are listed according to Irish custom; by importance rather than age. Thus the first child on the left in a family group may not be the oldest. Further, the main line of descent is usually through the child possessing the most talent and aggressiveness.

Most names in the body of the charts are Gaelic. I have followed the spelling given by the informant rather than text book spelling (on the assumption that the informant's family, and possibly others, considered the version offered to be correct). Some names in the body of the charts have one version of their English form shown in parentheses, as a comparison of Gaelic to English.

Dates do not indicate a specific time, such as birth or death, but rather a period during the traditional life of the person.

NOW - Visit your local library or genealogical society and read up on the antics, trials, tribulations and successes of your traditional ancestors.

Horn Head is a point of land on the northern coast
of County Donegal. Ships from Belfast and Derry
going to America could be watched as they passed by.
A cairn of stones at the viewpoint is said to have
been created by relatives who deposited a stone as
a ship passed carrying family members.

Billy Durning, farmer, poet, historian, owns a farm
on Horn Head and composed the following poem to his
fellow countrymen who have sought their fortunes in
foreign lands.

AN EMIGRANT'S FAREWELL

My native shores and green clad hills
    Are fading fast from view
The ship that bears me on my way
    Ploughs through the waters blue
With tearful eyes I backward gaze
    A parting look to share
As all the lofty mountains gray
    Have vanished into air

A moment now and all is blank
    As the land sank out of view
With grief gripped heart I do my part
    And wave a last adieu
The final glimpse of Erin gone
    I westward turn my gaze
Now sunbeams gleaming from the sky
    Are dancing on the waves

Ah! Fond memories of my old homestead
    I picture in my mind
The games we played, the sports we made
    With comrades true and kind
I cherish all my past career
    How swift the days rolled by
Now to my comrades one and all
    I bid a fond goodbye.

AN INDEX OF TRADITIONAL FAMILY RELATIONSHIPS

According to tradition, the Irish connected their ancestry to the Biblical genealogies in pre-Christian times.

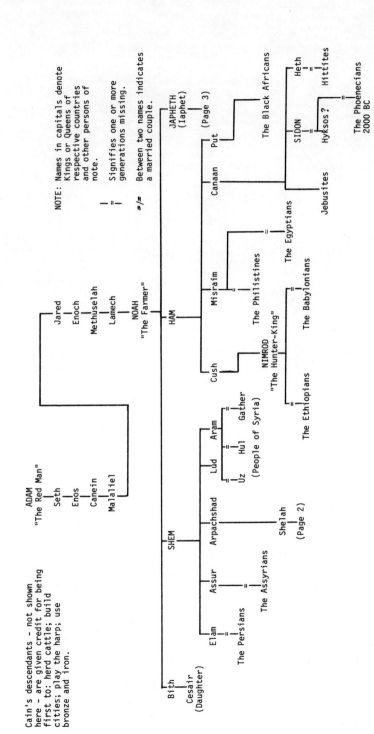

Cain's descendants - not shown here - are given credit for being first to: herd cattle; build cities; play the harp; use bronze and iron.

NOTE: Names in capitals denote Kings or Queens of respective countries and other persons of note.

—=—   Signifies one or more generations missing.

≠/=   Between two names indicates a married couple.

THE DESCENDANTS OF SHELAH
(From Page 1)

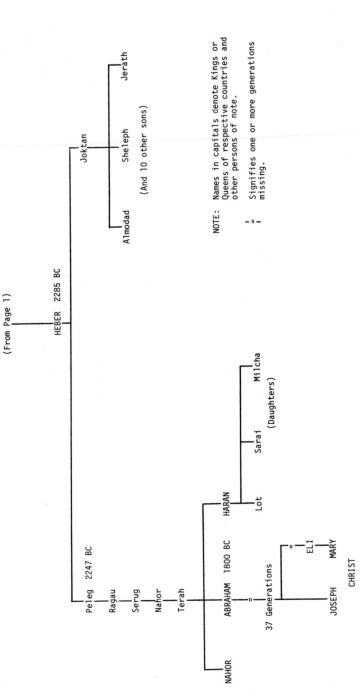

HEBER 2285 BC

Joktan

Almodad   Sheleph   Jerath

(And 10 other sons)

Peleg 2247 BC
Ragau
Serug
Nahor
Terah

NAHOR

ABRAHAM 1800 BC

HARAN

Lot   Sarai   Milcha

(Daughters)

37 Generations

ELI

JOSEPH   MARY

CHRIST

NOTE: Names in capitals denote Kings or
Queens of respective countries and
other persons of note.

= Signifies one or more generations
missing.

THE DESCENDANTS OF JAPHETH
(From Page 1)

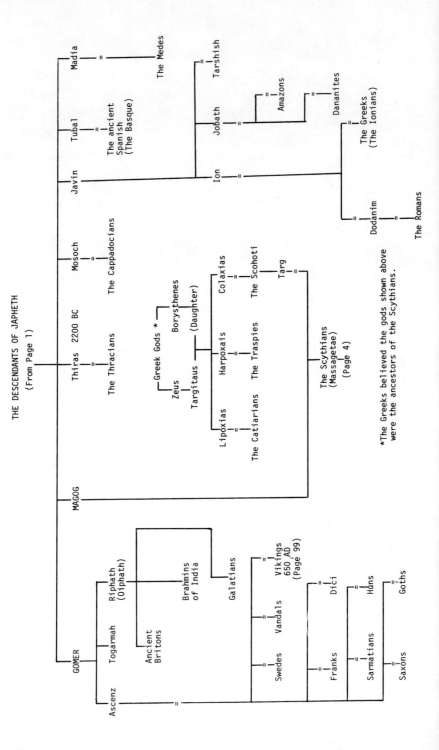

*The Greeks believed the gods shown above were the ancestors of the Scythians.

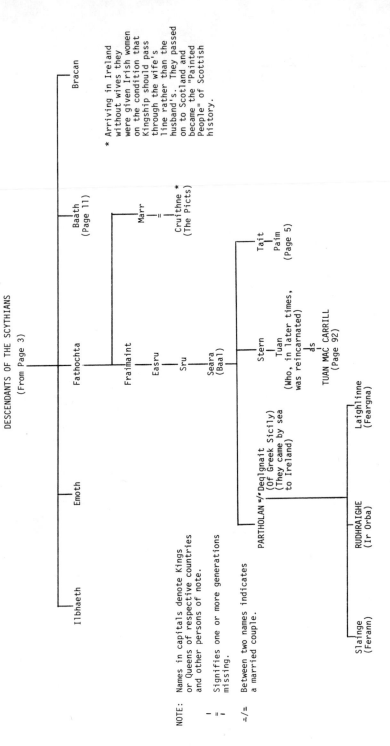

4

DESCENDANTS OF THE SCYTHIANS
(From Page 3)

Ilbhaeth

Emoth

Fathochta

Fraimaint

Easru

Sru

Seara
(Baal)

Stern

Tuan
(Who, in later times,
was reincarnated)

as

TUAN MAC CARRILL
(Page 92)

Baath
(Page 11)

Marr
=
Cruithne *
(The Picts)

Tait

Paim
(Page 5)

Bracan

* Arriving in Ireland
without wives they
were given Irish women
on the condition that
Kingship should pass
through the wife's
line rather than the
husband's. They passed
on to Scotland and
became the "Painted
People" of Scottish
history.

PARTHOLAN =/= Deqignait
(Of Greek Sicily)
(They came by sea
to Ireland)

RUDHRAIGHE
(Ir Orba)

Laighlinne
(Feargna)

Slainge
(Ferann)

NOTE: Names in capitals denote Kings
or Queens of respective countries
and other persons of note.

—
=   Signifies one or more generations
—   missing.

—/= Between two names indicates
a married couple.

5

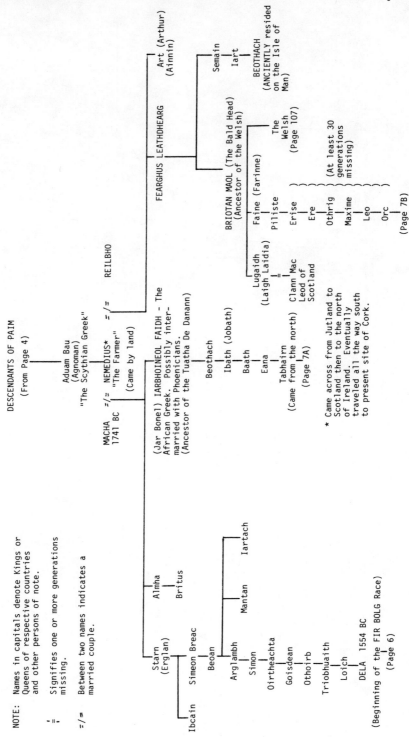

DESCENDANTS OF PAIM
(From Page 4)

NOTE: Names in capitals denote Kings or
Queens of respective countries
and other persons of note.

‑:‑   Signifies one or more generations
missing.

=/=   Between two names indicates a
married couple.

Aduam Bau
(Agnoman)
"The Scythian Greek"

MACHA   =/= NEMEDIUS*   =/= REILBHO
1741 BC   "The Farmer"
                 (Came by land)

(Jar Bonel) IARBHOINEOL FAIDH - The
African Greek. Possibly inter-
married with Phoenicians.
(Ancestor of the Tuatha De Danann)

Beothach

Ibath (Jobath)

Baath

Eana

Tabhairn
(Came from the north)
(Page 7A)

Lugaidh
(Laigh Laidia)
=
Clann Mac
Leod of
Scotland

* Came across from Jutland to
Scotland then to the north
of Ireland. Eventually
traveled all the way south
to present site of Cork.

FEARGHUS LEATHDHEARG

Art (Arthur)
(Ainnin)

Semain

Iart

BEOTHACH
(ANCIENTLY resided
on the Isle of
Man)

BRIOTAN MAOL (The Bald Head)
(Ancestor of the Welsh)

The
Welsh
(Page 107)

Faine (Farinne)

Piliste

Erise   )
)
Ere   )
) (At least 30
Othrig   ) generations
) missing)
Maxime   )
)
Leo   )
)
Orc   )
                 (Page 7B)

Starn
(Erglan)

Ibcain

Almha

Britus

Simeon Breac

Beoan

Arglambh

Mantan

Simon

Oirtheachta

Goisdean

Othoirb

Triobhuaith

Loich

DELA 1554 BC

(Beginning of the FIR BOLG Race)
(Page 6)

Iartach

6

DESCENDANTS OF DELA
(From Page 5)

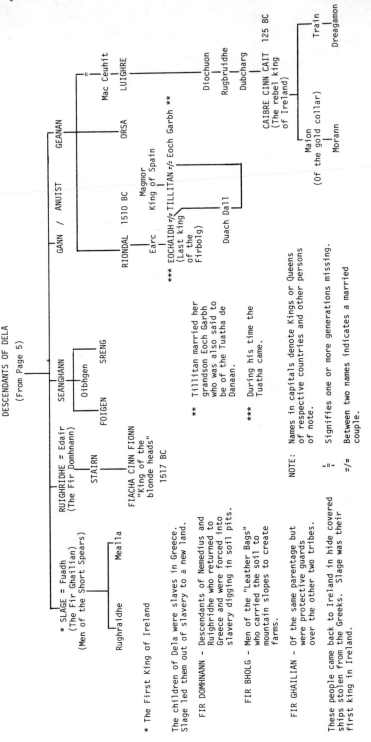

RUIGHRIDHE = Edair
(The Fir Domhnann)

* SLAGE = Fuadh
(The Fir Ghailian)
(Men of the Short Spears)

Rughraidhe   Mealla

STAIRN   FOIGEN   SRENG

FIACHA CINN FIONN
"King of the
blonde heads"
1517 BC

SEANGHANN   GANN / ANUIST   GEANAN

Oibhgen

RIONDAL 1510 BC

Magmor
King of Spain

Earc

EOCHAIDH =/= TILLITAN =/= Eoch Garbh **
(Last king
of the
Firbolg)

Duach Dall

ORSA   Mac Ceuhit

LUIGHRE

Diochuon

Rugbruidhe

Dubcharg

CAIBRE CINN CAIT 125 BC
(The rebel king
of Ireland)

Maion
(Of the gold collar)

Morann

Train

Dreagamon

* The First King of Ireland

The children of Dela were slaves in Greece.
Slage led them out of slavery to a new land.

FIR DOMHNANN - Descendants of Nemedius and
Ruighridhe who returned to
Greece and were forced into
slavery digging in soil pits.

FIR BHOLG - Men of the "Leather Bags"
who carried the soil to
mountain slopes to create
farms.

FIR GHAILIAN - Of the same parentage but
were protective guards
over the other two tribes.

These people came back to Ireland in hide covered
ships stolen from the Greeks. Slage was their
first king in Ireland.

** Tillitan married her
grandson Eoch Garbh
who was also said to
be of the Tuatha de
Danan.

*** During his time the
Tuatha came.

NOTE: Names in capitals denote Kings or Queens
of respective countries and other persons
of note.

= Signifies one or more generations missing.

=/= Between two names indicates a married
couple.

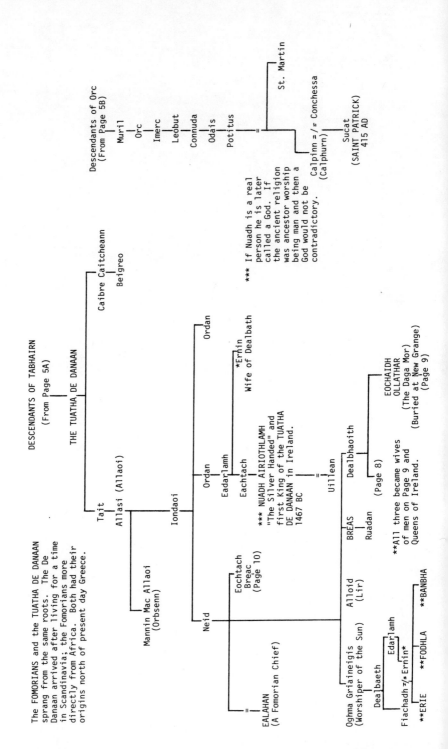

DESCENDANTS OF TABHAIRN
(From Page 5A)

THE TUATHA DE DANAAN

The FOMORIANS and the TUATHA DE DANAAN
sprang from the same roots. The De
Danaan arrived after living for a time
in Scandinavia; the Fomorians more
directly from Africa. Both had their
origins north of present day Greece.

Descendants of Orc
(From Page 5B)

Muril
Orc
Imerc
Leobut
Connuda
Odais
Potitus

St. Martin

=

Calpinn = / = Conchessa
(Calphurn)

Sucat
(SAINT PATRICK)
415 AD

*** If Nuadh is a real
person he is later
called a God. If
the ancient religion
was ancestor worship
being man and then a
God would not be
contradictory.

Tait

Allasi (Allaoi)

Caibre Caitcheann

Beigreo

Mannin Mac Allaoi
(Orbsenn)

Iondaoi

Neid

Ordan
Ordan
Eadar lamh
Eachtach

Ordan

*Erhin
Wife of Dealbath

Eochtach
Breac
(Page 10)

*** NUADH AIRIOTHLAMH
"The Silver Handed" and
first King of the TUATHA
DE DANAAN in Ireland.
1467 BC

Uillean

=

EALAHAN
(A Fomorian Chief)

=

Alloid
(Lir)

BREAS

Ruadan

Dealbhaoith

(Page 8)

EOCHAIDH
OLLATHAR
(The Daga Mor)
(Buried at New Grange)
(Page 9)

**All three became wives
of men on Page 9 and
Queens of Ireland.

Oghma Griaineigis
(Worshiper of the Sun)

Dealbaeth

Edar lamh

Fiachadh =/= Ernin*

**ERIE   **FODHLA   **BANBHA

8

DESCENDANTS OF DEALBHAOITH
(From Page 7)

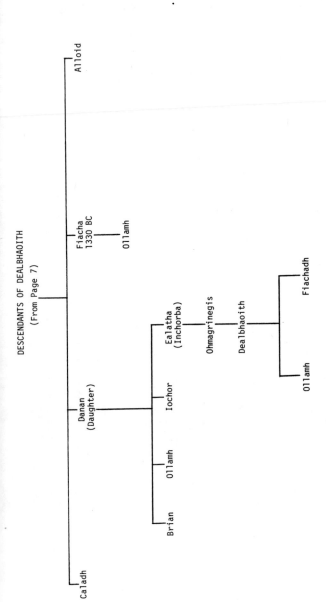

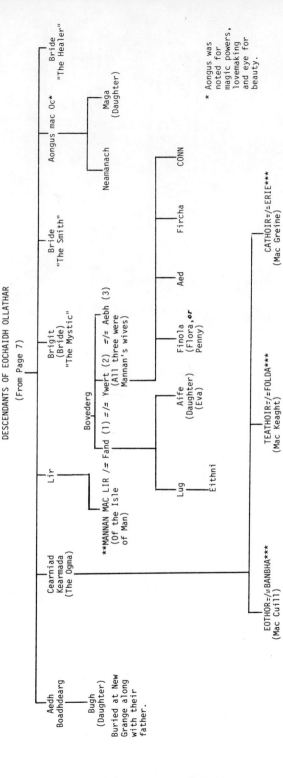

DESCENDANTS OF EOCHAIDH OLLATHAR

(From Page 7)

* Aongus was noted for magic powers, lovemaking and eye for beauty.

** Manawdyn Apllyr (Mannan mac Lir) was the fabled king of the Isle of Man; some ancients called it Ellan Vannin (Mannins Isle).

*** Banbha, Folda and Erie, three queens, ruled in rotation, Erie being on the throne when the Milesians arrived. They also are three poetic names for Ireland.

NOTE: Names in capitals denote Kings and Queens of respective countries and other persons of note.

=/=   Between two names indicates a married couple.

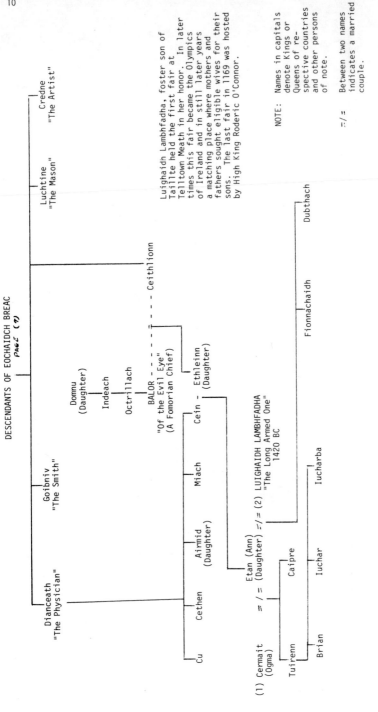

DESCENDANTS OF EOCHAIDCH BREAC
PAGE (?)

Dianceath
"The Physician"

Goibniu
"The Smith"

Luchtine
"The Mason"

Credne
"The Artist"

Domnu
(Daughter)

Indeach

Octrillach

BALOR - - - - : - - - - Ceithlionn
"Of the Evil Eye"
(A Fomorian Chief)

Cu

Cethen

Airmid
(Daughter)

Miach

Cein - Ethleinn
(Daughter)

Etan (Ann)
(1) Cermait   =/= (Daughter) =/= (2) LUIGHAIDH LAMBHFADHA
(Ogma)   "The Long Armed One"
                                    1420 BC

Tuirenn

Caipre

Iucharba

Fionnachaidh

Dubthach

Brian

Iuchar

Luighaidh Lambhfadha, foster son of
Tailite held the first fair at
Telltown Meath in her honor. In later
times this fair became the Olympics
of Ireland and in still later years
a matching place where mothers and
fathers sought eligible wives for their
sons. The last fair in 1169 was hosted
by High King Roderic O'Connor.

NOTE: Names in capitals
       denote Kings or
       Queens of re-
       spective countries
       and other persons
       of note.

=/=   Between two names
       indicates a married
       couple.

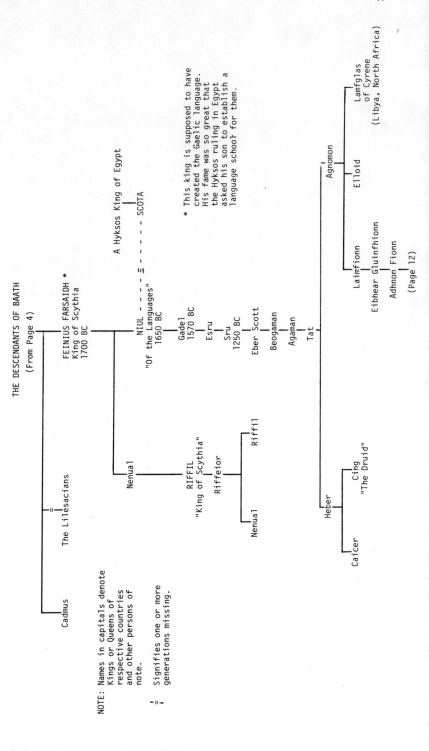

12

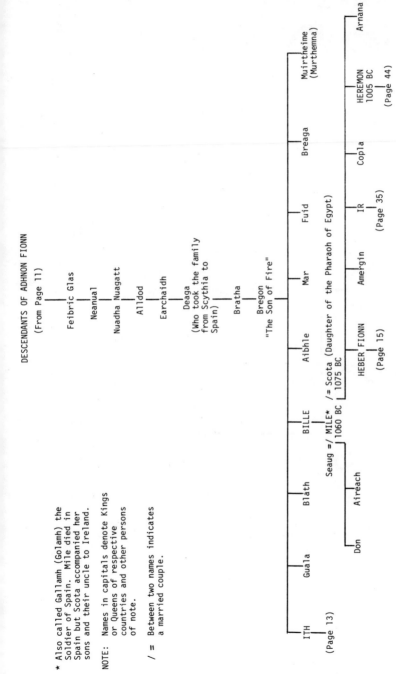

DESCENDANTS OF ADHNON FIONN
(From Page 11)

* Also called Gallamh (Golamh) the
Soldier of Spain. Mile died in
Spain but Scota accompanied her
sons and their uncle to Ireland.

NOTE: Names in capitals denote Kings
or Queens of respective
countries and other persons
of note.

/ = Between two names indicates
a married couple.

Feibric Glas

Neanual

Nuadha Nuagatt

Alldod

Earchaidh

Deaga
(Who took the family
from Scythia to
Spain)

Bratha

Bregon
"The Son of Fire"

ITH
(Page 13)

Guala   Blath   BILLE   Aibhle   Mar   Fuid   Breaga   Muirtheime
(Murthemna)

Seaug =/ MILE*   / = Scota (Daughter of the Pharaoh of Egypt)
1060 BC   1075 BC

Don
Aireach   HEBER FIONN   Amergin   IR   Copla   HEREMON
(Page 15)   (Page 35)   1005 BC
                                              (Page 44)   Arnana

DESCENDANTS OF ITH
(From page 12)

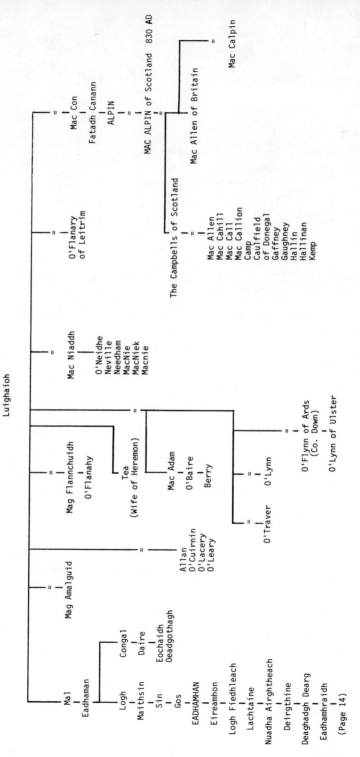

Luighaioh

Mal
Eadhaman

Logh
Maithsin
Sin
Gos

Congal
Daire
Eochaidh
Oeadgothagh

EADHAMHAN
Eireamhon
Logh Fiedhleach
Lachtaine
Nuadha Airghtheach
Deirgthine
Deaghadgh Dearg
Eadhamhraidh
(Page 14)

Mag Amalguid

Allan
O'Cuirnin
O'Lacery
O'Leary

Mag Flannchuidh
O'Flanahy

Tea
(Wife of Heremon)

Mac Adam
O'Baire
Berry

O'Traver   O'Lynn

O'Flynn of Ards
(Co. Down)

O'Lynn of Ulster

Mac Niaddh

O'Neidhe
Neville
Needham
MacNie
MacNiek
Macnie

O'Flanary
of Leitrim

The Campbells of Scotland

Mac Allen
Mac Cahill
Mac Call
Mac Callion
Camp
Caulfield
of Donegal
Gaffney
Gaughney
Hallin
Hallinan
Kemp

Mac Con
Fatadh Canann
ALPIN

MAC ALPIN of Scotland 830 AD

Mac Allen of Britain

Mac Calpin

14

DESCENDANTS OF EADHAMHRAIDH
(From page 13)

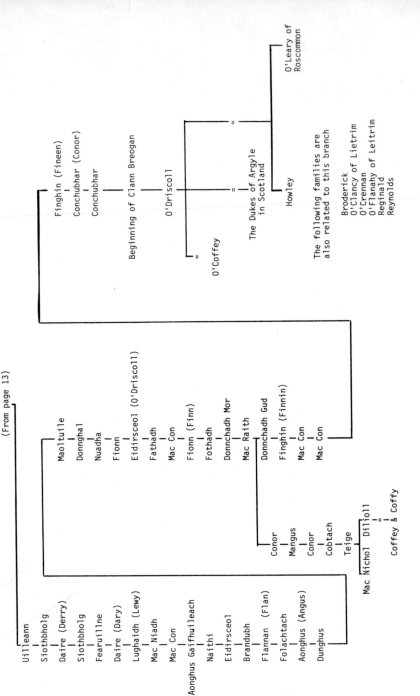

Uilleann
Siothbholg
Daire (Derry)
Siothbholg
Fearuillne
Daire (Dary)
Lughaidh (Lewy)
Mac Niadh
Mac Con
Aonghus Gaifhuileach
Naithi
Eidirsceol
Brandubh
Flannan (Flan)
Folachtach
Aonghus (Angus)
Dunghus

Maoltuile
Donnghal
Nuadha
Fionn
Eidirsceol (O'Driscoll)
Fathadh
Mac Con
Fionn (Finn)
Fothadh
Donnchadh Mor
Mac Raith
Donnchadh Gud
Finghin (Finnin)
Mac Con
Mac Con

Finghin (Fineen)
Conchubhar (Conor)
Conchubhar

Beginning of Clann Breogan

O'Driscoll

O'Coffey

The Dukes of Argyle
in Scotland

Howley

O'Leary of
Roscommon

Conor
Mangus
Conor
Cobtach
Teige

Mac Nichol Dilloll

Coffey & Coffy

The following families are
also related to this branch

Broderick
O'Clancy of Lietrim
O'Crennan
O'Flanahy of Leitrim
Reginald
Reynolds

15

DESCENDANTS OF HEBER FIONN
(From page 12)

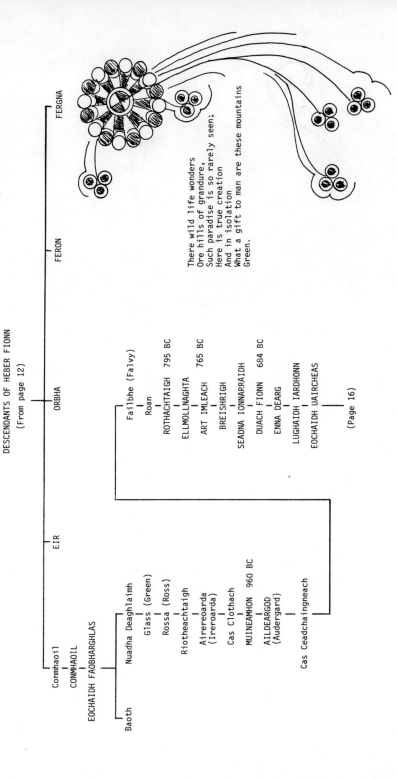

There wild life wonders
Ore hills of grandure,
Such paradise is so rarely seen;
Here is true creation
And in isolation
What a gift to man are these mountains
Green.

FERGNA

FERON

ORBHA

EIR

Conmhaoil
CONMHAOIL
EOCHAIDH FAOBHARGHLAS

Baoth

Nuadha Deaghlaimh

Glass (Green)

Rossa (Ross)

Riotheachtaigh

Airereoarda
(Ireroarda)

Cas Clothach

MUINEAMHON 960 BC

AILDEARGOD
(Audergard)

Cas Ceadchaingneach

Failbhe (Falvy)

Roan

ROTHACHTAIGH 795 BC

ELLMOLLNAGHTA

ART IMLEACH 765 BC

BREISHRIGH

SEADNA IONNARRAIDH

DUACH FIONN 684 BC

ENNA DEARG

LUGHAIDH IARDHONN

EOCHAIDH UAIRCHEAS

(Page 16)

16

DESCENDANTS OF EOCHAIDH OF UAIRCHEAS

(From page 15)

```
LUGHAIDH LAIMHDHEARG
       |
      ART            600 BC
       |
    OILILL FINN      585 BC ──── Cairbre Lusc
       |                          DUACH DALL   110 BC
 EOCHAIDH UARCEAS            (Duach Donn Dalltad Eaghaidh)
       |                      Eochaidh Fear Áine
 LUGHAIDH LAIGHDHE            MUREADHACH Muchna
       |
 REACHTAIDH RIGHDHEARG           MOFEIBhis
       |                       (Boadhafetbhis)
  Cobthach Caomb                  Loch Mor
       |                     (Luighneach Mor)
   MOGH CORB       357 BC     Enna Monchaoin
       |
   FEAR CORB                    Deirgthine
       |
 ADHAMAIR FOLTCHAOIN           Dearg (Goldy)
       |
  NIADH SEAGHAMAIN         Mogh Neid (The Magnificent)
       |
   IONNADMHAR      153 BC       (Page 17)
       |
 LUGHAIDH LUAIDHNE
```

When summer blossoms deck the fields
all clad in purple hue
The rugged mountains steep,
the lonely dell
I oft times watched the sun sink down,
upon the ocean blue
Then darted home as twilight swiftly fell.

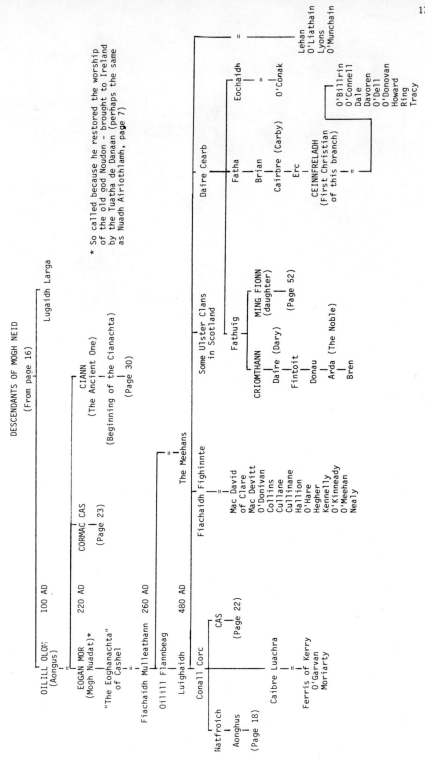

DESCENDANTS OF MOGH NEID
(From page 16)

18

DESCENDANTS OF AONGHUS
(From page 17)

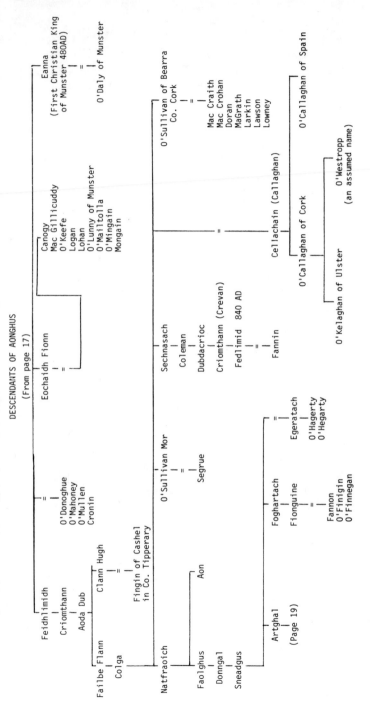

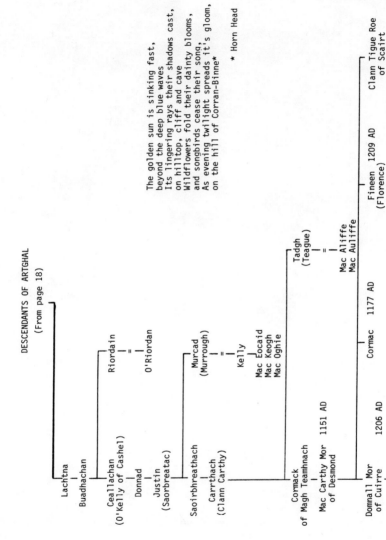

19

DESCENDANTS OF ARTGHAL
(From page 18)

Lachtna
Buadhachan
Ceallachan
(O'Kelly of Cashel)
Donnad
Justin
(Saorbreatac)

Riordain
=
O'Riordan

Saoirbhreathach
Carrthach
(Clann Carthy)

Murcad
(Murrough)
=
Kelly

Mac Eocaid
Mac Keogh
Mac Oghie

Cormack
of Magh Teamhnach
Mac Carthy Mor   1151 AD
of Desmond

Tadgh
(Teague)
=
Mac Aliffe
Mac Auliffe

Cormac   1177 AD

Domnall Mor
of Cuirre   1206 AD
(Page 20)

Fineen   1209 AD
(Florence)

Clann Tigue Roe
of Scairt

The golden sun is sinking fast,
beyond the deep blue waves
Its lingering rays their shadows cast,
on hilltop, cliff and cave
Wildflowers fold their dainty blooms,
and songbirds cease their song,
As evening twilight spreads it's gloom,
on the hill of Corran-Binne*

* Horn Head

20

DESCENDANTS OF DOMNALL MOR
(From page 19)

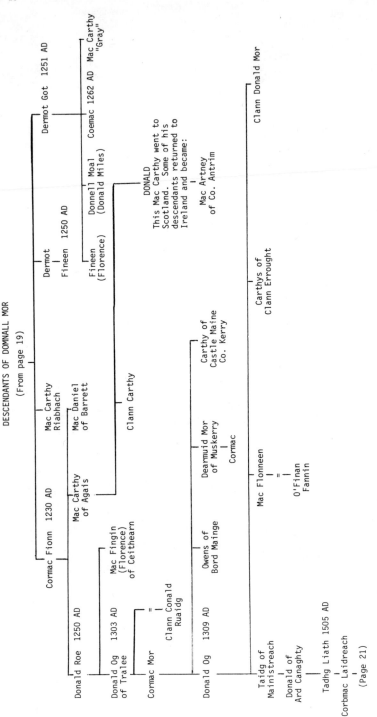

DESCENDANTS OF CORBMAC LAIDHREACH

(From page 20)

Donald of
Druimnin
|
=
|
Mac Carthy
Mac David
Mac Donagh
O'Meegan
O'Meehan

Owen

Donogh of
Ardeanagy

The following families are said
to be descendants of EOGHAN MOR
(page 17).

Mac Arthur
Mac Carter
O'Clerein
Collins
Collins of Sligo
O'Connell
O'Conor of Geinhim
O'Cremin
O'Cuillane
Drennan
Mac Elligott
O'Flannery
O'Fogerty
O'Heir
O'Kerwic
Kirby
O'Mecan
Tangney
Thornton

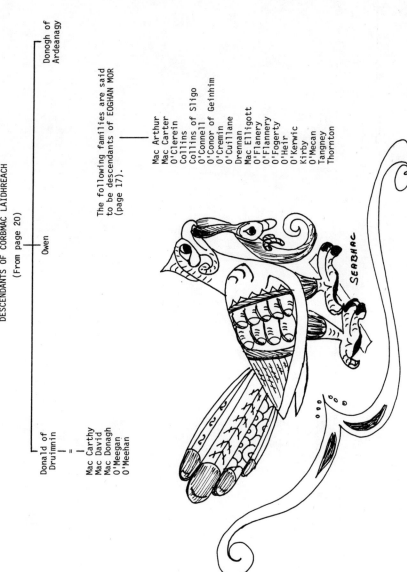

SEABHAC

22

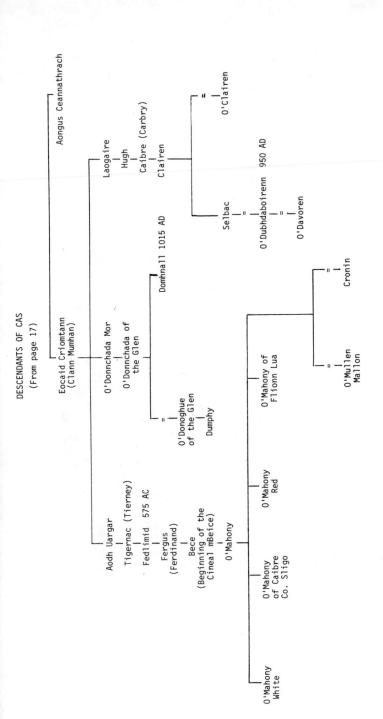

DESCENDANTS OF CAS
(From page 17)

Aongus Ceannathrach

Eocaid Criomtann
(Clann Mumhan)

Aodh Uargar

Tigernac (Tierney)

Fedlimid 575 AC

Fergus
(Ferdinand)

Bece
(Beginning of the
Cineal mBeice)

O'Mahony

O'Mahony
of Caibre
Co. Sligo

O'Mahony
White

O'Mahony
Red

O'Donnchada Mor

O'Donnchada of
the Glen

=
O'Donoghue
of the Glen

Dumphy

Domhnall 1015 AD

Laogaire

Hugh

Caibre (Carbry)

Clairen

Selbac

=
O'Dubhdaboirenn 950 AD

=
O'Davoren

=
O'Clairen

O'Mahony of
Flionn Lua

=
O'Mullen
Mallon

=
Cronin

DESCENDANTS OF CORMAC CAS
"Beginning of the Dal Cais"

(From page 17)

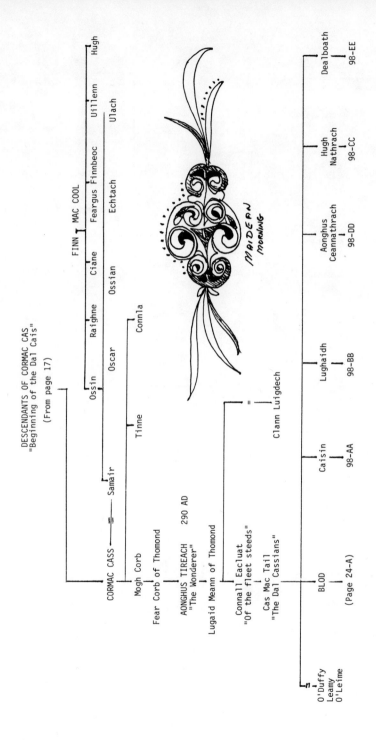

FINN MAC COOL

Ossin   Raighne   Ciane   Ossian   Feargus Finnbeoc   Uillenn   Hugh

Oscar   Connla   Echtach   Ulach

Tinne

CORMAC CASS ══ Samair

Mogh Corb

Fear Corb of Thomond

AONGHUS TIREACH   290 AD
"The Wonderer"

Lugaid Meann of Thomond

Connall Eacluat
"Of the fleet steeds"

Cas Mac Tail
"The Dal Cassians"

Clann Luigdech
═

BLOD   Caisin   Lughaidh   Aonghus Ceannnathrach   Hugh Nathrach   Dealboath
         98-AA   98-BB   98-DD   98-CC   98-EE

(Page 24-A)

O'Duffy
Leamy
O'Leime

MODERN MORNING

24

DESCENDANTS OF BLOD
(From page 23-A)

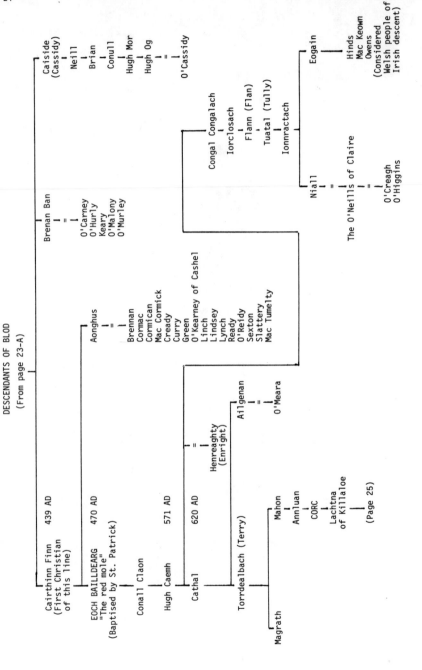

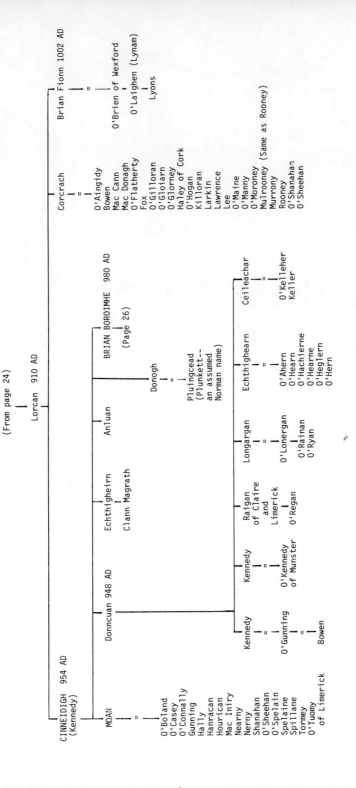

25

DESCENDANTS OF LACHTNA
(From page 24)

Lorcan 910 AD

CINNEIDIGH 954 AD
(Kennedy)

Brian Fionn 1002 AD

Corcrach

BRIAN BOROIMHE 980 AD
(Page 26)

Donncuan 948 AD

Anluan

Echthigheirn
Clann Magrath

=
O'Brien of Wexford
O'Laighen (Lynam)
    Lyons

=
O'Aingidy
Bowen
Mac Cann
Mac Donagh
O'Flatherty
Fox
O'Gilloran
O'Gloiarn
O'Glorney
Haley of Cork
O'Hogan
Killoran
Larkin
Lawrence
Lee
O'Maine
O'Manny
O'Moroney
Mulrooney (Same as Rooney)
Murrony
Rooney
O'Shanahan
O'Sheehan

Donogh
=
Pluingcead
(Plunkett--
an assumed
Norman name)

Ceileachar
=
O'Kelleher
Keller

MOAN
=
O'Boland
O'Casey
O'Connally
Gunning
Hally
Hanracan
Hourican
Mac Iniry
Nearny
Nerny
Shanahan
O'Sheehan
O'Spelain
Spelaine
Spillane
Tormey
O'Tuomy
of Limerick

Kennedy
=
O'Gunning
=
Bowen

Kennedy
=
O'Kennedy
of Munster

Raigan
of Claire
and
Limerick
O'Regan

Longargan
=
O'Lonergan
O'Rainan
O'Ryan

Echthighearn
=
O'Ahern
O'Hearn
O'Hachierne
O'Hearne
O'Heglern
O'Hern

26

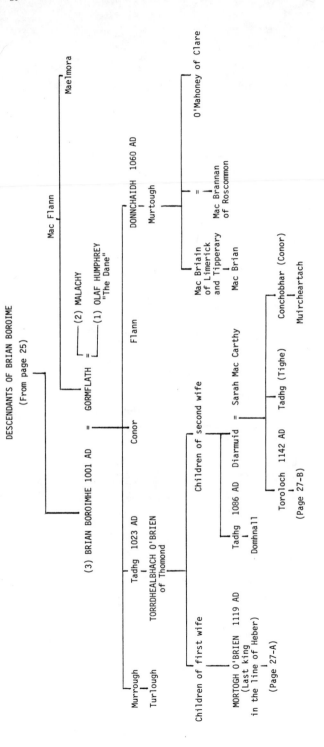

DESCENDANTS OF BRIAN BOROIME
(From page 25)

Mac Flann

Maelmora

GORMFLATH
(2) MALACHY
(1) OLAF HUMPHREY "The Dane"

(3) BRIAN BOROIMHE 1001 AD

Conor

Flann

DONNCHAIDH 1060 AD

Murtough

O'Mahoney of Clare

Mac Brannan of Roscommon

Mac Briain of Limerick and Tipperary

Mac Brian

Children of second wife

Diarmuid = Sarah Mac Carthy

Tadhg (Tighe)

Conchobhar (Conor)

Muircheartach

Toroloch 1142 AD

(Page 27-B)

Tadhg 1086 AD

Domhnall

Murrough

Turlough

Tadhg 1023 AD

TORRDHEALBHACH O'BRIEN of Thomond

Children of first wife

MORTOGH O'BRIEN 1119 AD
(Last king in the line of Heber)

(Page 27-A)

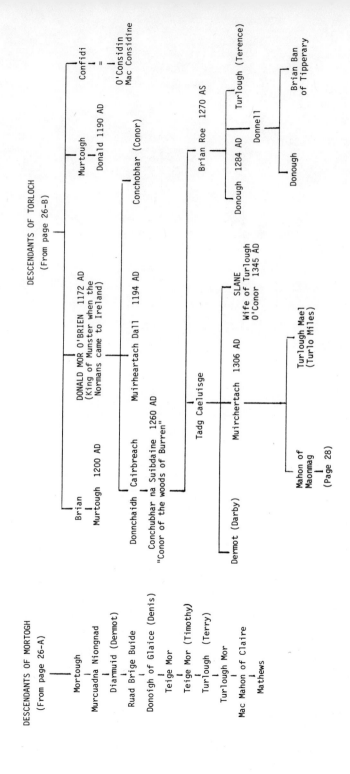

DESCENDANTS OF TORLOCH
(From page 26-B)

DESCENDANTS OF MORTOGH
(From page 26-A)

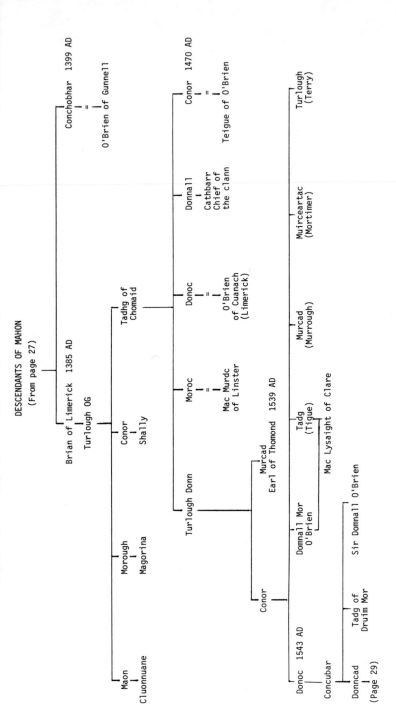

DESCENDANTS OF MAHON
(From page 27)

DESCENDANTS OF DONNCAD

(From page 28)

"The" O'Brien
of Thomond

Henry O'Brien
Earl of Thomond   1646 AD

The following descend from the O'Briens above:

Bryant
Canning
O'Concannon
Kennyon

The following families descend from CORMAC CASS (page 23) but are not assigned a specific place in the genealogy:

Arthur	Mac Bride	Brodie	Mac Brody	Brolly
O'Collopy	Coning	Curneen	Mac Curtin	O'Diff
Mac Duffie	Duffy	O'Duhrig	O'Durack	O'Halloran
Hickey	Hinnigan	Kearney	Kilbride (a branch of Mac Bride)	
O'Nolan	Noonan	O'Nunan	Rider	Ryder

The above list is an example of how confusing Irish Genealogy can be at times: Arthur, the first name on the list is probably an "assumed" Irish name. The English "King Arthur" comes to mind and has no connection here. The origin of the name in Ireland is quite probably Norse, if so then an Irish descendant of Cormac Cass "assumed" the name for his family out of admiration for the original bearer or under political or religious pressure, which, on more than one occasion caused an Irishman to take an "English sounding" name.

The importance of a knowledge of the family homeland is demonstrated by the name Mac Grath. This family has a long association with the O'Briens of Thomond, however, a separate and well known family of the same name can be found in counties Fermanagh and Donegal.

DESCENDANTS OF CIANN, SON OF MOGH NEID, LINE OF EOGHAIN MOR

(From page 17)

Tadhg (Teague)

Cormac an Chaile
=
Mac Colgan
Mac Cormack
Cormican
Culligan

Cormac Gaileang
(Clan Luighne)

O'Hara
of Antrim

O'Casie
Cassidy
Cochrane
Flanagan

=
Mac Alary of Antrim
Clark
Mac Cleary

O'Devan
Downs
O'Duaine
Dwain
O'Gadra
O'Grady of Cork
O'Hara of Sligo
Hooke

=
O'Connor of Derry
(Glengevin)

Connla

Fionnachta

Feigh
=
O'Flannagain of
Cineal Arra
Co. Tipperary

EOCHAIDH FAOBHEARGHLAS
(Sabhormnich)

Carrol
O'Carroll of Ely
Co. Offaly
Cochrane
Dulanty

Athchu
Lughaidh (Lewy)
Fathaidh
Feidhlimidh (Phelim)
Donn Cuinn
(Page 31-B)

Iomchadh

Sabharn
Earc
Righdhearg of Eile
Drui
Amhruadh
Meacher
Tal
(Page 31-A)

Fionnachtach
=
Lachtnain
Loftus

O'Maher
O'Meagher
(The Siol Meachair)

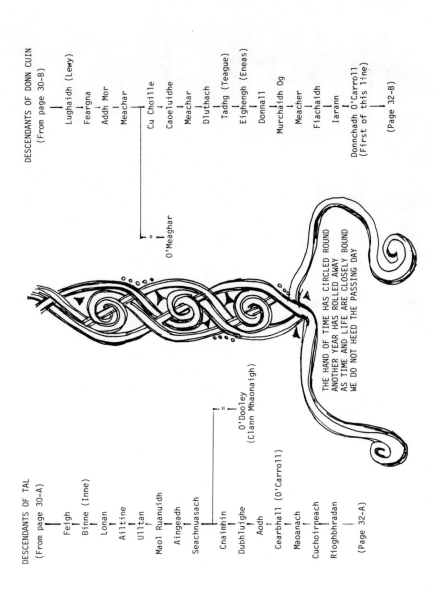

DESCENDANTS OF DONN CUIN
(From page 30-B)

Lughaidh (Lewy)

Feargna

Addh Mor

Meachar

Cu Choille

Caoeluidhe

Meachar

Dluthach

Tadhg (Teague)

Eighengh (Eneas)

Donnall

Murchaidh Og

Meacher

Fiachaidh

Iarann

Donnchadh O'Carroll
(First of this line)

(Page 32-B)

= O'Meaghar

THE HAND OF TIME HAS CIRCLED ROUND
ANOTHER YEAR HAS ROLLED AWAY
AS TIME AND LIFE ARE CLOSELY BOUND
WE DO NOT HEED THE PASSING DAY

DESCENDANTS OF TAL
(From page 30-A)

Feigh

Binne (Inne)

Lonan

Ailtine

Ulltan

Maol Ruanuidh

Aingeadh

Seachnusasach

Cnaimhin

Dubhluighe

Aodh

Cearbhall (O'Carroll)

Maoanach

Cuchoirpeach

Rioghbhradan

(Page 32-A)

= O'Dooley
(Clann Mhaonaigh)

32

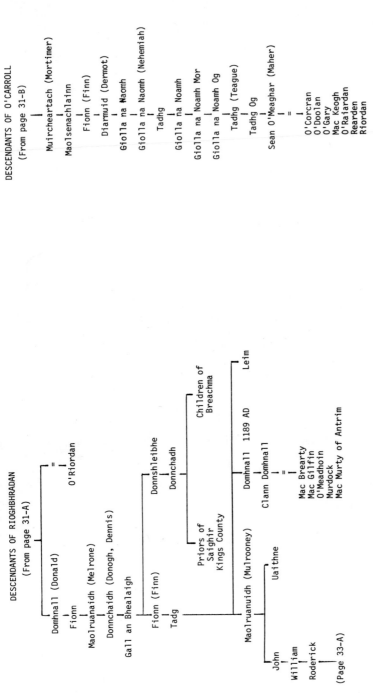

DESCENDANTS OF O'CARROLL
(From page 31-B)

Muircheartach (Mortimer)

Maolsenachlainn

Fionn (Finn)

Diarmuid (Dermot)

Giolla na Naomh

Giolla na Naomh (Nehemiah)

Tadhg

Giolla na Noamh

Giolla na Noamh Mor

Giolla na Noamh Og

Tadhg (Teague)

Tadhg Og

Sean O'Meaghar (Maher)
=

O'Corcran
O'Doolan
O'Gary
Mac Keogh
O'Raiardan
Rearden
Riordan

DESCENDANTS OF RIOGHBHRADAN
(From page 31-A)

Domhnall (Donald)
=
O'Riordan

Fionn

Maolruanaidh (Melrone)

Donnchaidh (Donogh, Dennis)

Gall an Bhealaigh

Fionn (Finn)

Tadg

Priors of
Saighir
Kings County

Donnshleibhe

Donnchadh

Children of
Breachma

Domhnall 1189 AD   Leim

Clann Domhnall
=

Mac Brearty
Mac Gilfin
O'Meadhoin
Murdock
Mac Murty of Antrim

Maolruanuidh (Mulrooney)

Uaithne

John

William

Roderick

(Page 33-A)

33

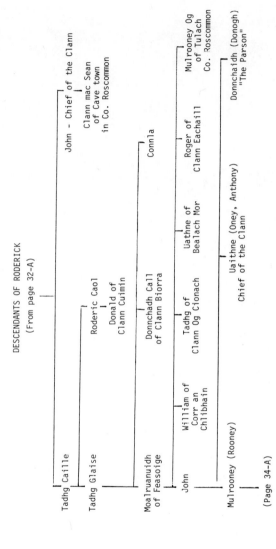

DESCENDANTS OF RODERICK
(From page 32-A)

Tadhg Caille

John - Chief of the Clann

Clann mac Sean
of Cave town
in Co. Roscommon

Tadhg Glaise

Roderic Caol

Donald of
Clann Cuimin

Moalruanuidh
of Feasoige

Connla

Donnchadh Call
of Clann Biorra

William of
Corr an
Chlibhain

Tadhg of
Clann Og Cionach

Uathne of
Bealach Mor

Roger of
Clann Eachaill

Mulrooney Og
of Tulach
Co. Roscommon

John

Uaithne (Oney, Anthony)
Chief of the Clann

Donnchaidh (Donogh)
"The Parson"

Mulrooney (Rooney)

(Page 34-A)

34

DESCENDANTS OF MULROONEY
(From page 33-A)

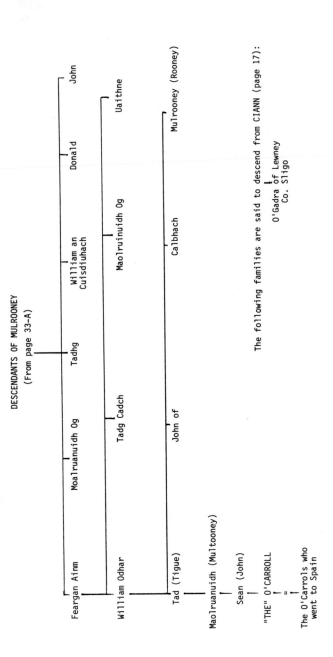

The following families are said to descend from CIANN (page 17):

Feargan Ainm

Moalruanuidh Og — Tadhg — William an Cuisdiuhach — Donald — John

William Odhar — Tadg Cadch — Maolruinuidh Og — Uaithne

Tad (Tigue) — John of — Calbhach — Mulrooney (Rooney)

Maolruanuidh (Multooney)

Sean (John)

"THE" O'CARROLL
=
The O'Carrols who
went to Spain

O'Gadra of Lewney
Co. Sligo

DESCENDANTS OF IR
(From page 12)

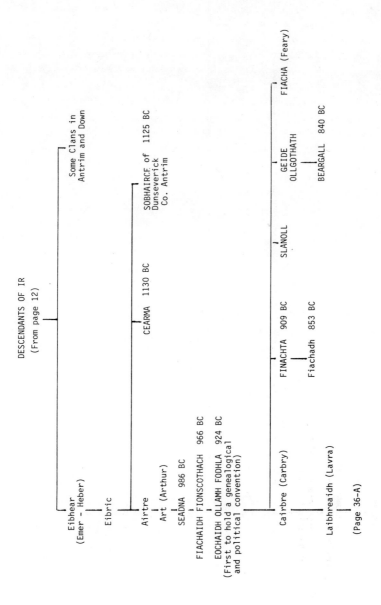

Eibhear
(Emer – Heber)

Eibric

Airtre
Art (Arthur)
SEADNA   986 BC
FIACHAIDH FIONSCOTHACH   966 BC
EOCHAIDH OLLAMH FODHLA   924 BC
(First to hold a genealogical
and political convention)

Cairbre (Carbry)

Laibhreaidh (Lavra)

(Page 36-A)

Some Clans in
Antrim and Down

CEARMA   1130 BC

SOBHAIRC.F. of   1125 BC
Dunseverick
Co. Antrim

FINACHTA   909 BC

Fiachadh   853 BC

SLANOLL

GEIDE
OLLGOTHATH

BEARGALL   840 BC

FIACHA (Feary)

36

DESCENDANTS OF LAIBHRAIDH
(From page 35)

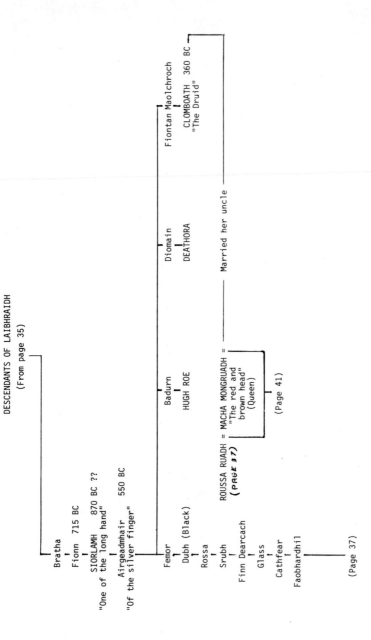

Bratha
|
Fionn 715 BC
|
SIORLAMH 870 BC ??
"One of the long hand"
|
Airgeadmhair 550 BC
"Of the silver finger"

Femor
|
Dubh (Black)
|
Rossa
|
Srubh
|
Finn Dearcach
|
Glass
|
Cathfear
|
Faobhardhil

(Page 37)

Badurn
|
HUGH ROE

Diomain
|
DEATHORA

Fiontan Maolchroch
|
CLOMBOATH 360 BC
"The Druid"

ROUSSA RUADH = MACHA MONGRUADH =
(PAGE 37)   "The red and
               brown head"
               (Queen)

Married her uncle

(Page 41)

37

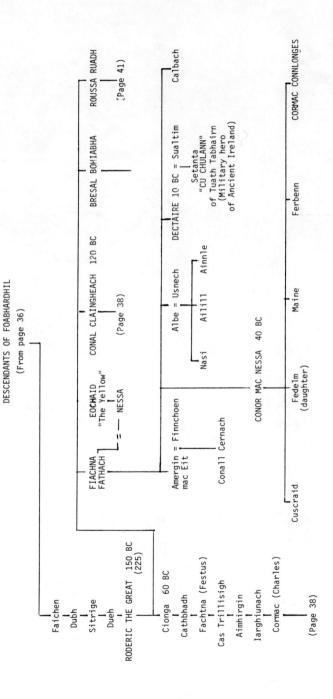

DESCENDANTS OF FOABHARDHIL
(From page 36)

38

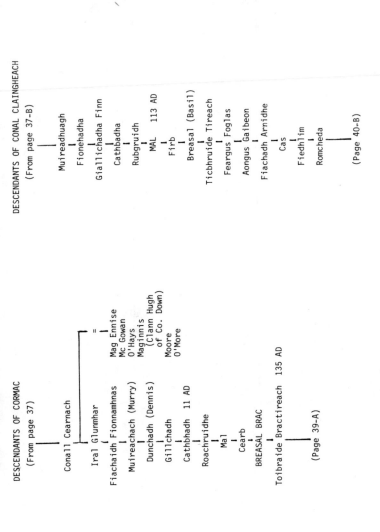

DESCENDANTS OF CORMAC
(From page 37)

Conall Cearnach
Iral Glunmhar
Fiachaidh Fionnamhnas
Muireachach (Murry)
Dunchadh (Dennis)
Gillchadh
Cathbhadh 11 AD
Roachruidhe
Mal
Cearb
BREASAL BRAC
Toibraide Bractireach 135 AD

(Page 39-A)

=

Mag Ennise
Mc Gowan
O'Hays
Maginnis
(Clann Hugh
of Co. Down)
Moore
O'More

DESCENDANTS OF CONAL CLAINGHEACH
(From page 37-B)

Muireadhuagh
Fionehadha
Giallichadha Finn
Cathbadha
Rubgruidh
MAL   113 AD
Firb
Breasal (Basil)
Ticbhruide Tireach
Feargus Foglas
Aongus Gaibeon
Fiachadh Arnidhe
Cas
Fiedhlim
Romcheda

(Page 40-B)

DESCENDANTS OF TOIBRAIDE BRACTIREACH
(From page 38)

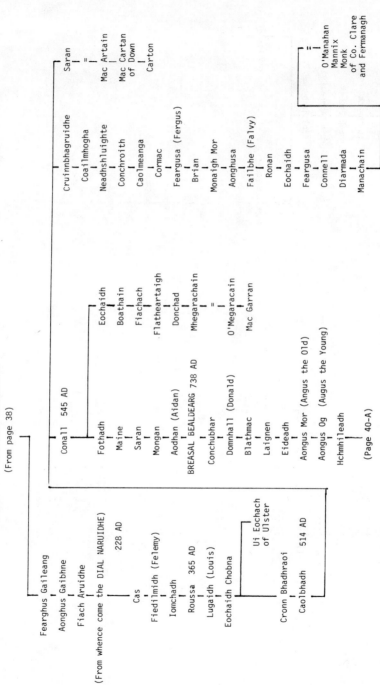

Fearghus Gaileang
Aonghus Gaibhne
Fiach Aruidhe
(From whence come the DIAL NARUIDHE)
Cas   228 AD
Fiedilmidh (Felemy)
Iomchadh
Roussa   365 AD
Lugaidh (Louis)
Eochaidh Chobna

Ui Eochach
of Ulster

Cronn Bhadhraoi
Caolbhadh   514 AD

Conall   545 AD

Fothadh
Maine
Saran
Mongan
Aodhan (Aidan)
BREASAL BEALDEARG 738 AD
Conchubhar
Domhall (Donald)
Blathmac
Laignen
Eideadh
Aongus Mor (Angus the Old)
Aongus Og (Augus the Young)
Hchmhileadh
(Page 40-A)

Eochaidh
Boathain
Fiachach
Flatheartaigh
Donchad
Mhegarachain
=
O'Megaracain
Mac Garran

Cruinmbhagruidhe
Coailmhogha
Neadhshluighte
Conchroith
Caolmeanga
Cormac
Feargusa (Fergus)
Brian
Monaigh Mor
Aonghusa
Failbhe (Falvy)
Ronan
Eochaidh
Feargusa
Connell
Diarmada
Manachain

Saran
=
Mac Artain
Mac Cartan
of Down
Carton

=
O'Manahan
Mannix
Monk
of Co. Clare
and Fermanagh

40

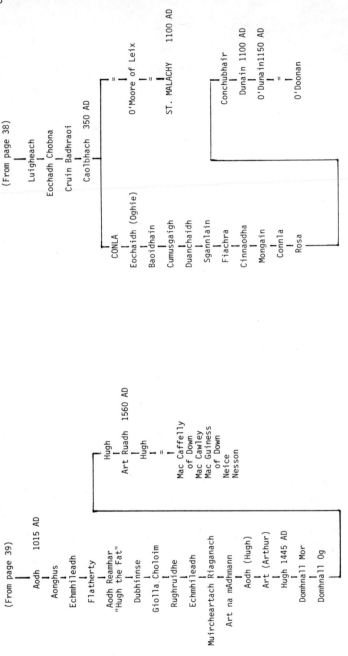

DESCENDANTS OF TOMCHEDA
(From page 38)

Luigheach
Eochadh Chobna
Cruin Badhraoi
Caolbhach 350 AD

CONLA
Eochaidh (Oghie) ═ O'Moore of Leix
Baoidhain
Cumusgaigh ═ ST. MALACHY 1100 AD
Duanchaidh
Sgannlain
Fiachra
Cinnaodha
Mongain
Connla
Rosa

Conchubhair
Dunain 1100 AD
O'Dunain 1150 AD
═
O'Doonan

DESCENDANTS OF HMCHMHILEADH
(From page 39)

Aodh   1015 AD
Aonghus
Echmhileadh
Flatherty
Aodh Reamhar "Hugh the Fat"
Dubhinnse
Giolla Choloim
Rughruidhe
Echmhileadh
Muircheartach Riaganach
Art na mAdhmann
Aodh (Hugh)
Art (Arthur)
Hugh 1445 AD
Domhnall Mor
Domhnall Og

Hugh
Art Ruadh 1560 AD
Hugh ═ Mac Caffelly of Down
Mac Cawley
Mac Guiness of Down
Neice
Nesson

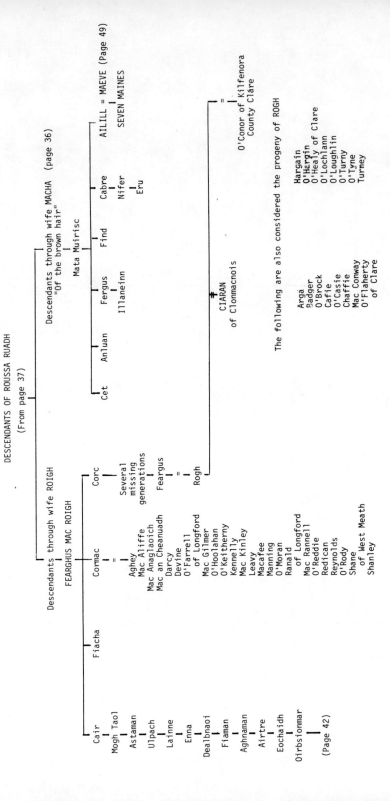

DESCENDANTS OF ROUSSA RUADH
(From page 37)

Descendants through wife ROIGH

FEARGHUS MAC ROIGH

Descendants through wife MACHA (page 36)
"Of the brown hair"

Mata Muirisc

Cet   Anluan   Fergus   Find   Cabre   AILILL = MAEVE (Page 49)
              Illaneinn   Nifer   SEVEN MAINES
                                Eru

CIARAN
of Clonmacnois

= O'Conor of Kilfenora
   County Clare

The following are also considered the progeny of ROGH

Arga   Hargain
Badger   O'Hergin
O'Brock   O'Healy of Clare
Cafie   O'Lochlann
O'Casle   O'Loughlin
Chaffie   O'Turny
Mac Conway O'Tyne
O'Flaherty Turney
of Clare

Cair
Mogh Taol
Astaman
Ulpach
Lainne
Enna
Dealbnaoi
Fiaman
Aghnaman
Airtre
Eochaidh
Oirbsionmar

(Page 42)

Fiacha

Cormac
=
Aghey
Mac Aliffe
Mac Anaglaoich
Mac an Cheanuadh
Darcy
Devine
O'Farrell
of Longford
Mac Gilmer
O'Hoolahan
O'Keitherny
Kennelly
Mac Kinley
Leavy
Macafee
Manning
O'Moran
Ranald
of Longford
Mac Rannell
O'Reddie
Redican
Reynolds
O'Rody
Shane
of West Meath
Shanley

Corc

Several
missing
generations
Feargus
=
Rogh

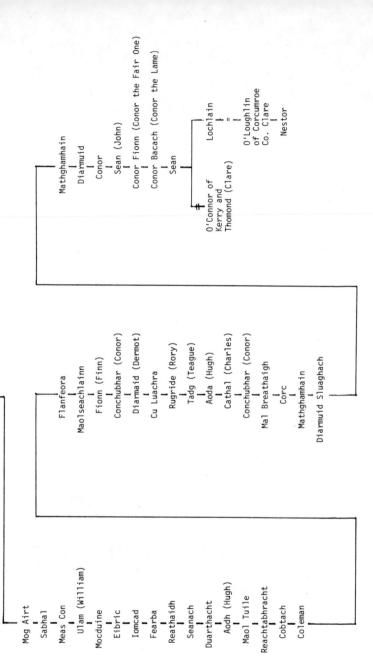

DESCENDANTS OF OIRBSIONMAR
(From page 41)

43

DESCENDANTS OF FEARGHUS MAC ROIGH
son of Roussa Ruadh
(From page 41)

Prior to 1100 AD most family members could recite the entire genealogy of their clan beginning with themselves and going back to the first king of their branch. The importance of clann relationships, although under attack by the Normans, remained alive through oral recitation. The great shifts of population following the 1600's so disrupted family relationships that genealogies were jumbled within two or three generations as far as the common man was concerned. Many leading families, with their books lost or burned suffered a similar fate. Some families retained only the memory of their most important ancestor. Thus the families listed below, although they do not have a fixed place in the table, never-the-less claim Fearghus Mac Roigh as their ancestor:

Brosnan	Cahill	Carrolan	O'Carlin	Colter
Corless	Coulter	O'Curry	O'Dorey	O'Duan
O'Dunlevy	Downs	Mac Eochadh	Fitzpatrick	Mac Gilligan
		of Linster		
Mac Granuill	O'Hanby	O'Hargain	O'Heochy	O'Kearney
			(changed to	
			Mac Dunlevy	
O'Laverty	O'Lawler	O'Lyn	O'Laynam	Lynch
Manning	O'Moora	O'Moore of Leix	O'Neachach	O'Scanlon
Smith of Down	O'Tierny	Mac Ward		

DESCENDANTS OF HEREMON SON OF MILE
(From page 12)

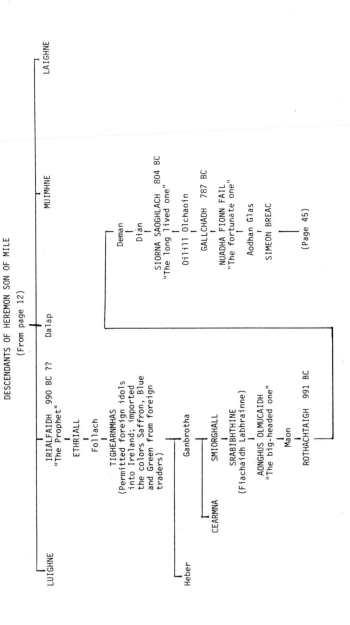

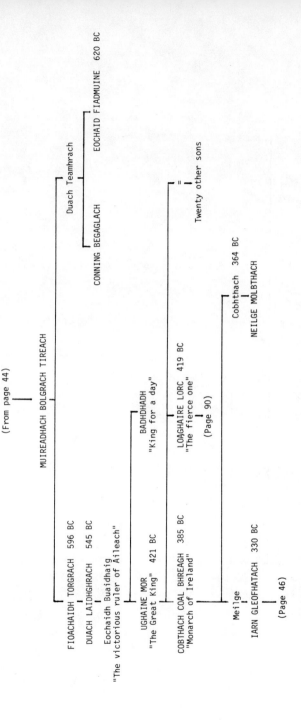

DESCENDANTS OF SIMEON BREAC
(From page 44)

MUIREADHACH BOLGRACH TIREACH

Duach Teamhrach

CONNING BEGAGLACH   EOCHAID FIADMUINE   620 BC

=

Twenty other sons

Cobhthach   364 BC

NEILGE MOLBTHACH

FIOACHAIDH TORGRACH   596 BC
DUACH LAIDHGHRACH   545 BC
Eochaidh Buaidhaig
"The victorious ruler of Aileach"

BADHDHADH
"King for a day"

LOAGHAIRE LORC   419 BC
"The fierce one"
(Page 90)

UGHAINE MOR
"The Great King"   421 BC

COBTHACH COAL BHREAGH   385 BC
"Monarch of Ireland"

Meilge
IARN GLEOFHATACH   330 BC

(Page 46)

45

46

DESCENDANTS OF IARN GLEOFHATACH
(From page 45)

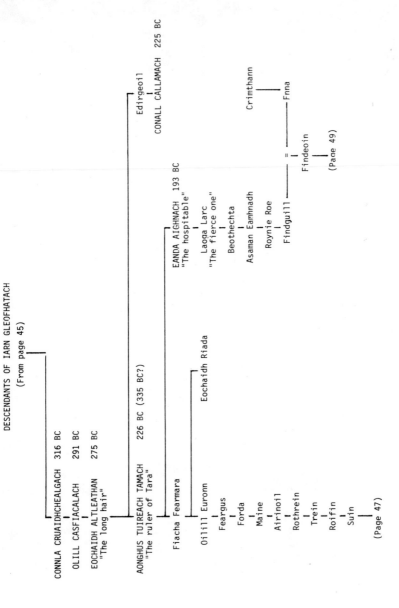

CONNLA CRUAIDHCHEALGACH   316 BC

OLILL CASFIACALACH   291 BC

EOCHAIDH ALTLEATHAN   275 BC
"The long hair"

AONGHUS TUIREACH TAMACH   226 BC (335 BC?)
"The ruler of Tara"

Fiacha Fearmara

Oilill Euronn   Eochaidh Riada

Feargus

Forda

Maine

Airinoil

Rothrein

Trein

Roifin

Suin

(Page 47)

EANDA AIGHNACH 193 BC
"The hospitable"

Laoqa Larc
"The fierce one"

Beothechta

Asaman Eamhnadh

Roynie Roe

Findguill

Findeoin

=

(Page 49)

Edirgeoil

CONALL CALLAMACH   225 BC

Crimthann

Fnna

DESCENDANTS OF SUIN
(From page 46)

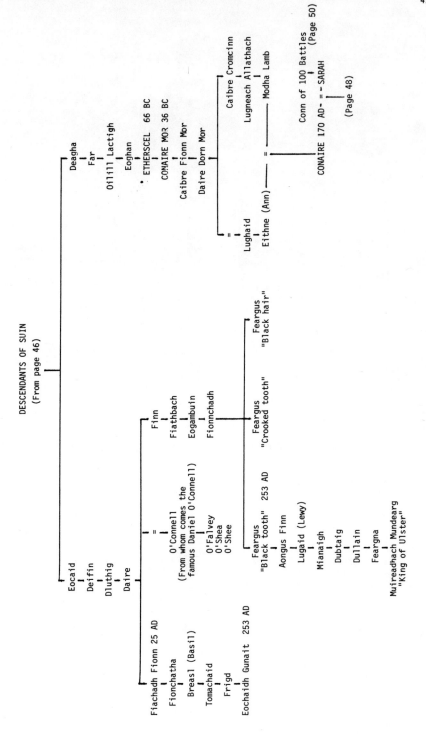

Eocaid
Deifin
Dluthig
Daire

Deagha
Far
Oilill Lactigh
Eoghan
• ETHERSCEL 66 BC
COMAIRE MOR 36 BC
Caibre Fionn Mor
Daire Dorn Mor

Caibre Cromcinn
Lugneach Allathach
Modha Lamb

= Conn of 100 Battles (Page 50)

CONAIRE 170 AD = SARAH

(Page 48)

=
Lughaid
Eithne (Ann)

O'Connell
(From whom comes the
famous Daniel O'Connell)

O'Falvey
O'Shea
O'Shee

Finn
Fiathbach
Eogambuin
Fionnchadh

Feargus
"Crooked tooth"

Feargus
"Black hair"

Fiachadh Fionn 25 AD
Fionchatha
Breasl (Basil)
Tomachaid
Frigd
Eochaidh Gunait 253 AD

Feargus
"Black tooth" 253 AD
Aongus Finn
Lugaid (Lewy)
Mianaigh
Dubtaig
Dullain
Feargna

Muireadhach Mundearg
"King of Ulster"

48

DESCENDANTS OF CONAIRE

(From page 47)

CAIBRE RIADA

EARC (Erk) 503 AD

Lorn   Feargus   Angus

The Dial Riada
of Scotland and Ulster

Fiachaidh Cathmhaol

Eochaidh (Oghie, Hogie)

Eagar

Fiolimi

Seanchormac

Fiedhlimidh (Felix)

Aonghus

Aislingtheach

Aonghus Feart

CAIBRE MUSC
=

Mac Adam
Mac Anawe
Mac Cadden of Armagh
Mac Caw of Cavin
O'Coirc
Mac Conave
Mac Egan
Mac Enawe
Ford
Kennelly
Kinnavy
Mac Kinnawe
Kineavy
Malone
Mac Neely *

* see page 49

Musgoin

CAIBRE BAISCINN
(Clann Baschaoin of Clare)
=
=
O'Failbe of Desmond
Co. Clare

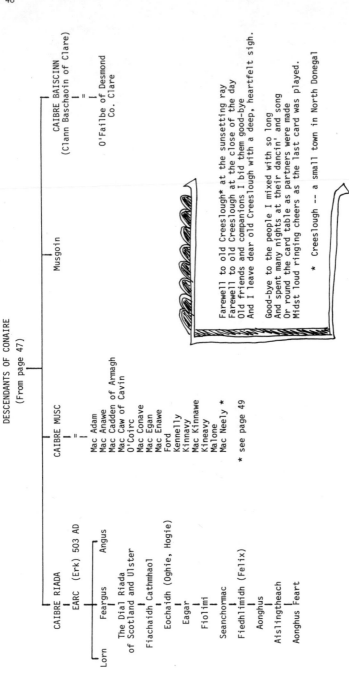

Farewell to old Creeslough* at the sunsetting ray
Farewell to old Creeslough at the close of the day
Old friends and companions I bid them good-bye
And I leave dear old Creeslough with a deep, heartfelt sigh.

Good-bye to the people I mixed with so long
And spent many nights at their dancin' and song
Or round the card table as partners were made
Midst loud ringing cheers as the last card was played.

* Creeslough -- a small town in North Donegal

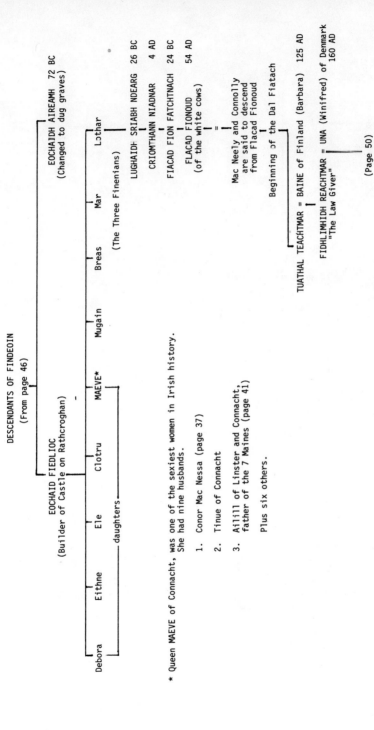

DESCENDANTS OF FINDEOIN
(From page 46)

EOCHAID FIEDLIOC
(Builder of Castle on Rathcroghan)

daughters

Debora Eithne Ele Clotru MAEVE* Mugain Breas Mar Lothar

(The Three Finenians)

EOCHAIDH AIREAMH 72 BC
(Changed to dug graves)

LUGHAIDH SRIABH NDEARG 26 BC

CRIOMTHANN NIADNAR 4 AD

FIACAD FION FATCHTNACH 24 BC

FLACAD FIONOUD 54 AD
(of the white cows)
=

Mac Neely and Connolly
are said to descend
from Flacad Fionoud

Beginning of the Dal Fiatach

TUATHAL TEACHTMAR = BAINE of Finland (Barbara) 125 AD

FIDHLIMHIDH REACHTMAR = UNA (Winifred) of Denmark
"The Law Giver"   160 AD

(Page 50)

* Queen MAEVE of Connacht, was one of the sexiest women in Irish history.
  She had nine husbands.

  1. Conor Mac Nessa (page 37)

  2. Tinue of Connacht

  3. Ailill of Linster and Connacht,
     father of the 7 Maines (page 41)

     Plus six others.

50

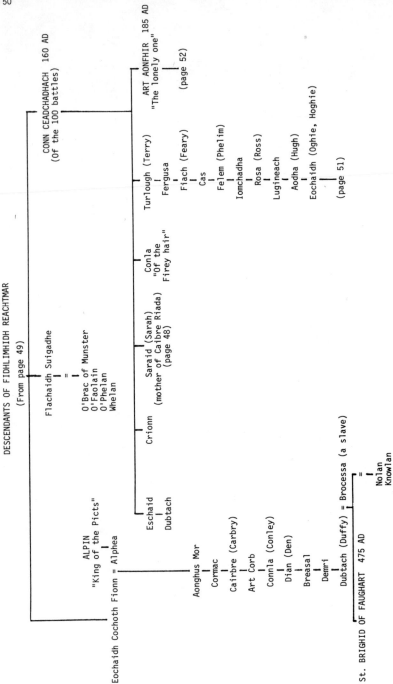

DESCENDANTS OF FIDHLIMHIDH REACHTMAR
(From page 49)

Eochaidh Cochoth Fionn = Alphea

ALPIN
"King of the Picts"

Flachaidh Suigadhe
=
O'Brac of Munster
O'Faolain
O'Phelan
Whelan

CONN CEADCHADHACH 160 AD
(Of the 100 battles)

ART AONFHIR 185 AD
"The lonely one"

(page 52)

Turlough (Terry)
|
Fergusa

Fiach (Feary)

Cas

Felem (Phelim)

Iomchadha

Rosa (Ross)

Lugineach

Aodha (Hugh)

Eochaidh (Oghie, Hoghie)

(page 51)

Conla
"Of the
Firey hair"

Saraid (Sarah)
(mother of Caibre Riada)
(page 48)

Crionn

Eschaid
|
Dubtach

Aonghus Mor

Cormac

Cairbre (Carbry)

Art Corb

Connla (Conley)

Dian (Den)

Breasal

Demri

Dubtach (Duffy) = Brocessa (a slave)
=
Nolan
Knowlan

St. BRIGHID OF FAUGHART 475 AD

DESCENDANTS OF EOCHAIDH
(From page 50)

Cruinn (Cuan)
Caolohadh
Conla (Conley)
Eochaidh (Hoghie)
Fiachach (Feary)

Conga mac Eochaidh
Cinnfhaoilidh
Baoidhain
Duanchaidh mhic Comusgaigh
Sgannlain
Cinnaodha mac Fiachra
Mongain
Connla (Conley)
Rosa
Conchubhar (Conor)
=
Clann Dunain

Flaitheartaigh
=
Mac Giolla Laisir

Clann Mhegarachain

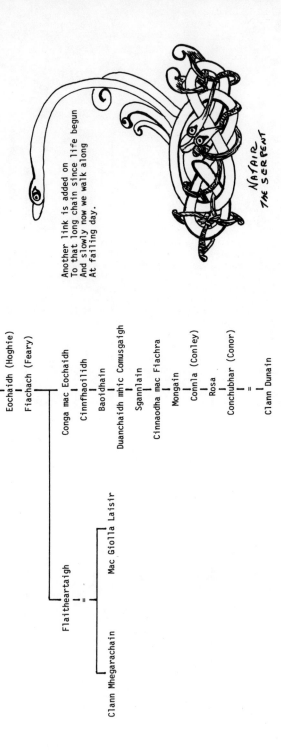

Another link is added on
To that long chain since life begun
And slowly now we walk along
At failing day.

NATAIR
THE SERPENT

52

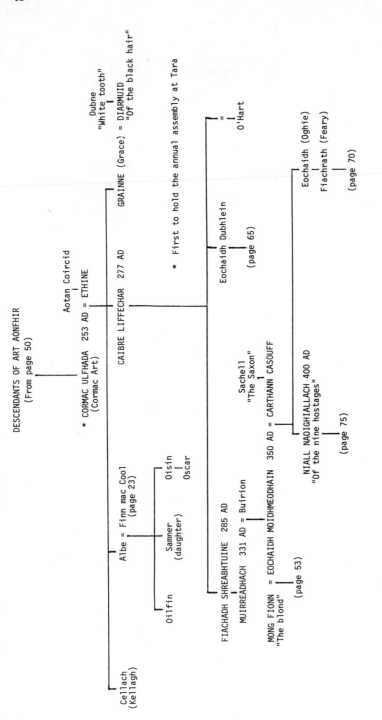

DESCENDANTS OF ART AONFHIR
(From page 50)

Aotan Coircid

Dubne "White tooth"

* CORMAC ULFHADA 253 AD = ETHINE
(Cormac Art)

CAIBRE LIFFECHAR 277 AD

GRAINNE (Grace) = DIARMUID "Of the black hair"

* First to hold the annual assembly at Tara

Eochaidh Dubhlein
(page 65)

= O'Hart

Eochaidh (Oghie)
Fiachrath (Feary)
(page 70)

Cellach (Kellagh)

Albe = Finn mac Cool
(page 23)

Oisin
Oscar

Oilfin

Samner
(daughter)

FIACHADH SHREABHTUINE 285 AD
MUIRREADHACH 331 AD = Buirion

Sachell "The Saxon"

MONG FIONN = EOCHAIDH MOIDHMEODHAIN 350 AD = CARTHANN CASOUFF
"The blond"
(page 53)

NIALL NAOIGHIALLACH 400 AD
"Of the nine hostages"
(page 75)

53

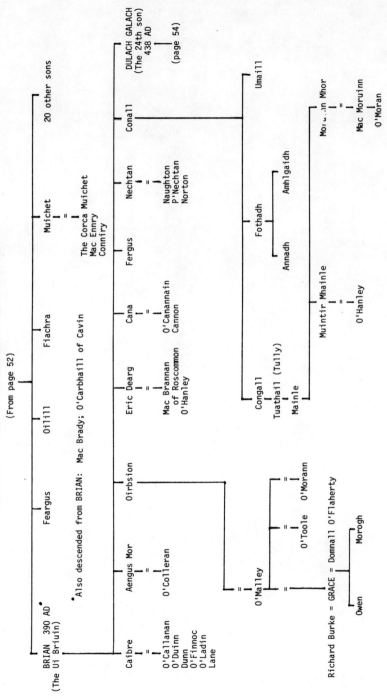

DESCENDANTS OF EOCHAIDH MOIDHMEODHAIN THROUGH MONG FIONN
(From page 52)

54

DESCENDANTS OF DUACH GALACH
(From page 53)

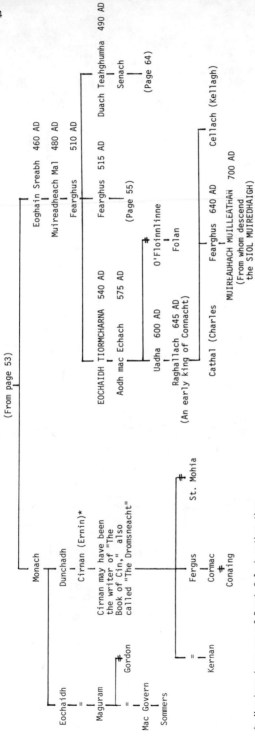

Monach

Dunchadh

Cirnan (Ernin)*

Cirnan may have been
the writer of "The
Book of Cin," also
called "The Dromsneacht"

Eoghain Sreabh   460 AD

Muireadheach Mal   480 AD

Fearghus   510 AD

Fearghus   515 AD

(Page 55)

Duach Teaghumha   490 AD

Senach

(Page 64)

EOCHAIDH TIORMCHARNA   540 AD

Aodh mac Echach   575 AD

Uadha   600 AD

Raghallach   645 AD
(An early king of Connacht)

O'Floinnlinne

Folan

Cathal (Charles

Fearghus   640 AD

MUIREAUHACH MUILLEÁTHÁN   700 AD
(From whom descend
the SIOL MUIREDHAIGH)

(Page 57)

Cellach (Kellagh)

Eochaidh

=

Maguram

=

Gordon

Mac Govern

Sommers

Fergus

Cormac

Conaing

St. Mohia

=

Kernan

* May have been son of Duach Galach rather than
great-grandson. He was said to have been one
of the great poets, historians and geneologists
of Ancient Ireland.

DESCENDANTS OF FEARGUS
(From page 54)

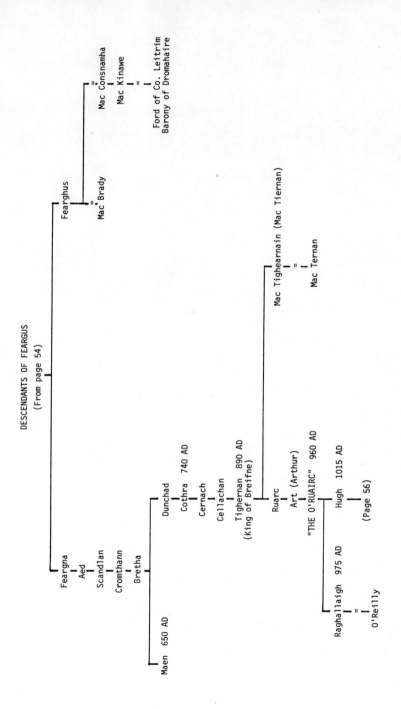

Feargna
Aed
Scandlan
Cromthann
Bretha

Maen 650 AD

Dunchad
Cothra 740 AD
Cernach
Cellachan
Tighernan 890 AD
(King of Breifne)

Ruarc
Art (Arthur)
"THE O'RUAIRC" 960 AD
Hugh 1015 AD
(Page 56)

Raghallaigh 975 AD
=
O'Reilly

Fearghus
=
Mac Brady

=
Mac Consnamha
=
Mac Kinawe
Ford of Co. Leitrim
Barony of Dromahaire

Mac Tighearnain (Mac Tiernan)
=
Mac Ternan

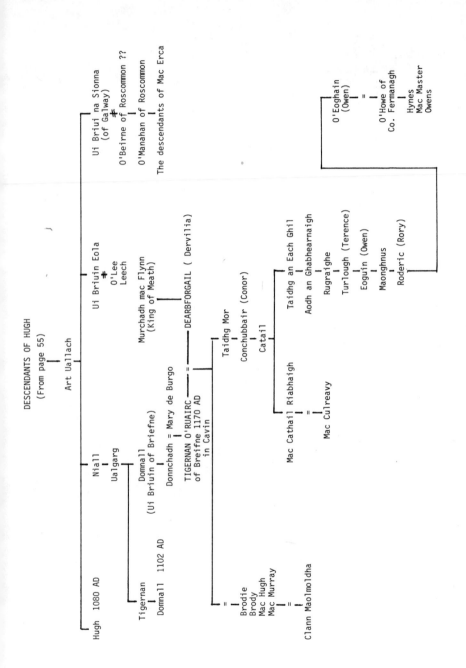

DESCENDANTS OF HUGH
(From page 55)

Art Uallach

Hugh 1080 AD

Niall
Ualgarg

Domnall
(Ui Briuin of Briefne)

Tigernan
Domnall 1102 AD

Donnchadh = Mary de Burgo

TIGERNAN O'RUAIRC ———— DEARBFORGAIL (Dervilia)
of Breifne 1170 AD
in Cavin

=
Brodie
Brody
Mac Hugh
Mac Murray

=
Clann Maolmoldha

Mac Cathail Riabhaigh

=
Mac Culreavy

Taidhg Mor

Conchubbair (Conor)

Catail

Taidhg an Each Ghil

Aodh an Ghabhearnaigh

Rugraighe

Turlough (Terence)

Eoguin (Owen)

Maonghnus

Roderic (Rory)

Ui Briuin Eola

O'Lee
Leech

Murchadh mac Flynn
(King of Meath)

Ui Briui na Sionna
(of Galway)

O'Beirne of Roscommon ??

O'Manahan of Roscommon

The descendants of Mac Erca

O'Eoghain
(Owen)

=
O'Howe of
Co. Fermanagh

Hynes
Mac Master
Owens

57

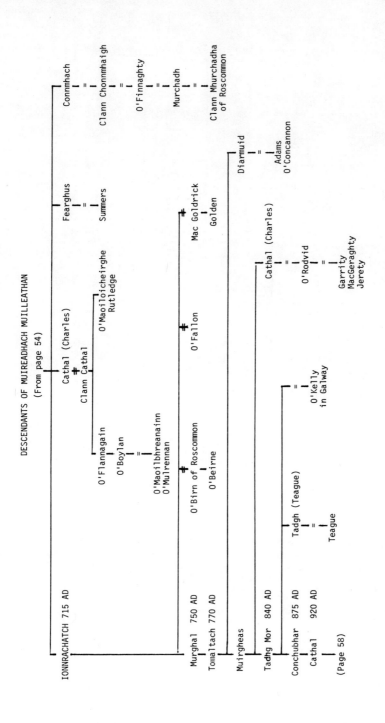

DESCENDANTS OF MUIREADHACH MUILLEATHAN
(From page 54)

58

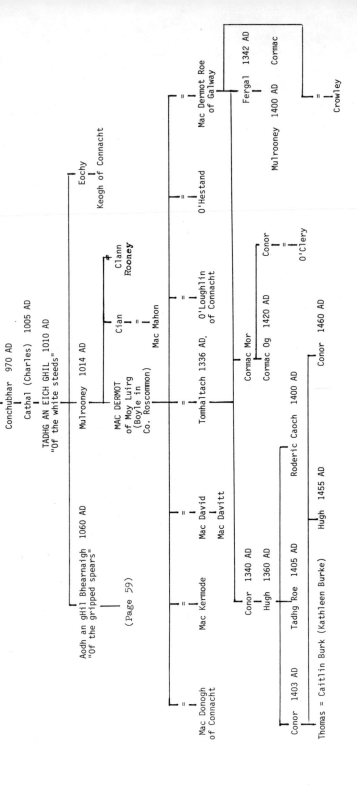

DESCENDANTS OF CATHAL
(From page 57)

Tadhg 950 AD

Conchubhar 970 AD

Cathal (Charles) 1005 AD

TADHG AN EICH GHIL 1010 AD
"Of the white steeds"

Mulrooney 1014 AD

Eochy

Keogh of Connacht

MAC DERMOT
of Moy Luirg
(Boyle in
Co. Roscommon)

Cian
=
Mac Mahon

Clann
Rooney

Aodh an gHil Bhearnaigh 1060 AD
"Of the gripped spears"

(Page 59)

Tomhaltach 1336 AD

O'Loughlin
of Connacht

O'Hestand

Mac Dermot Roe
of Galway

Fergal 1342 AD

Cormac

Mulrooney 1400 AD

=
Crowley

Mac Kermode

Mac David
Mac Davitt

Cormac Mor

Cormac Og 1420 AD

Conor
=
O'Clery

Mac Donogh
of Connacht

Conor 1340 AD
Hugh 1360 AD

Conor 1403 AD

Tadhg Roe 1405 AD

Roderic Caoch 1400 AD

Hugh 1455 AD

Conor 1460 AD

Thomas = Caitlin Burk (Kathleen Burke)

DESCENDANTS OF AODH AN GHILBHEARNAIGH
(From page 58)

RUIDIHRI NA SOIGHE BUIDHE 1118 AD

TOIRDHEALBHACH MOR O'CONOR 1150 AD

Niall Aithclerech

Donald

CONOR O'CONOR
(King of Dublin)

Gilbert
Changed his surname

Nogent

Brian of
Brifney

Dubcoblaigh

O'Eogain

Conor Roe

BRIAN LUIGHNEACH 1181 AD

(Page 60)

Magnus

Brian an Dori

Mac Manus of
Roscommon

Mac Bryan
Mac Brine
Bruen
O'Bradin

Diarmit

Clann Conaifne

Cathal Roe

Hugh 1310 AD

Rory   1316 AD
Tadhg   1374 AD

CATHAL CROIBHOHEARG
1220 AD

(Page 61)

Muirchertach
Muimnech   1210 AD

Clann Muirchertaig

Conor the Red 1245 AD

Manus   1280 AD

RUADHE
O'CONCHUBHAIR 1150 AD

(Page 62)

Dearbhfhorghail
(Dervilia)
Daughter

Donald
Riabach

Conor

Hugh O'Donnell

Daimaid
Brian of
the Oak

Hugh Ballach
1300 AD

Aodh Dall 1136
(Hugh the blind)

Maelsechlainn

Fingen

Connchad

O'Mallone
O'Gilbey
O'Gilvy

60

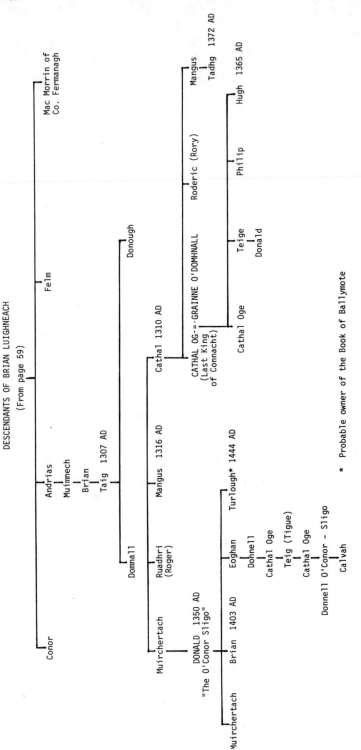

DESCENDANTS OF BRIAN LUIGHNEACH
(From page 59)

Conor

Felm

Andrias
Muimnech
Brian
Taig 1307 AD

Mac Morrin of
Co. Fermanagh

Domnall

Donough

Muirchertach

Ruadhri
(Roger)

Mangus 1316 AD

Cathal 1310 AD

Roderic (Rory)

Mangus
Tadhg 1372 AD

DONALD 1350 AD
"The O'Conor Sligo"

Turlough* 1444 AD

CATHAL OG = GRAINNE O'DOMHNALL
(Last King
of Connacht)

Cathal Oge

Teige
Donald

Philip

Hugh 1365 AD

Muirchertach

Brian 1403 AD

Eoghan
Donnell
Cathal Oge
Teig (Tigue)
Cathal Oge
Donnell O'Conor - Sligo
Calvah

* Probable owner of the Book of Ballymote

61

DESCENDANTS OF CATHAL CROIBHDHEARG
(From page 59)

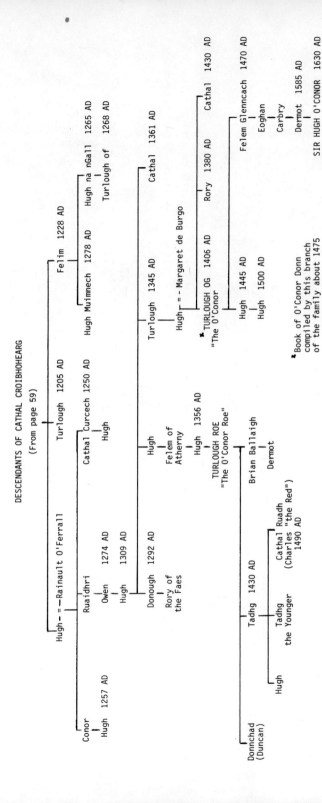

Mac Kiernan and Mac Tiernan also believed
to be a branch of the O'Conors

62

DESCENDANTS OF RODERIC O'CONOR *
(From page 59)

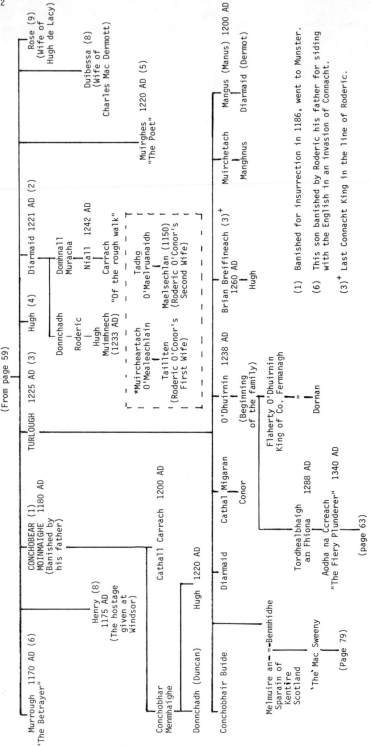

(1) Banished for insurrection in 1186, went to Munster.

(6) This son banished by Roderic his father for siding with the English in an invasion of Connacht.

(3)+ Last Connacht King in the line of Roderic.

63

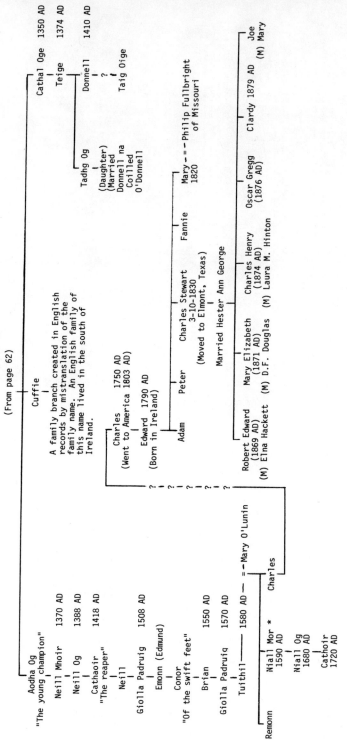

DESCENDANTS OF AODHA NA CCREACH
(From page 62)

A family branch created in English records by mistranslation of the family name. An English family of this name lived in the south of Ireland.

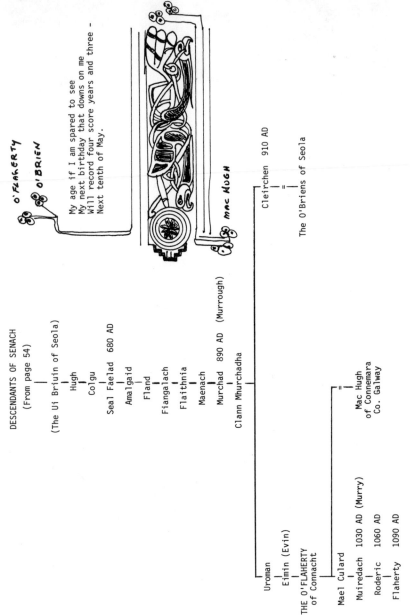

O'FLAHERTY

O'BRIEN

My age if I am spared to see
My next birthday that downs on me
Will record four score years and three -
Next tenth of May.

MAC HUGH

DESCENDANTS OF SENACH

(From page 54)

(The Ui Briuin of Seola)

Hugh

Colgu

Seal Faelad   680 AD

Amalgaid

Fland

Fiangalach

Flaithnia

Maenach

Murchad   890 AD   (Murrough)

Clann Mhurchadha

Cleirchen   910 AD

=

The O'Briens of Seola

Uroman

Eimin (Evin)

THE O'FLAHERTY of Connacht

Mael Culard

Muiredach   1030 AD   (Murry)

Roderic   1060 AD

Flaherty   1090 AD

=

Mac Hugh
of Connemara
Co. Galway

65

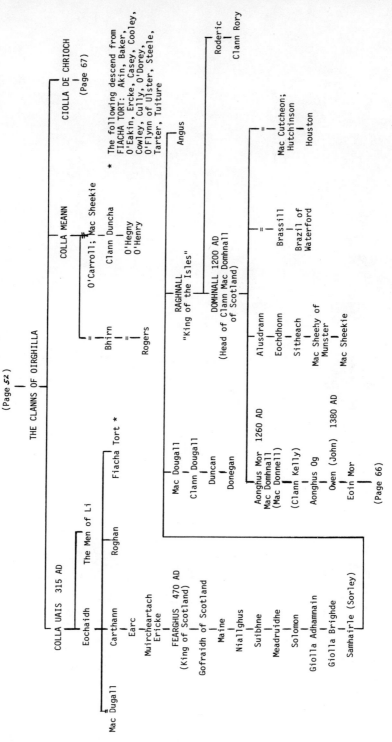

DESCENDANTS OF EOCHAIDH DUBHLEIN
(Page 52)

THE CLANNS OF OIRGHILLA

66

DESCENDANTS OF EOIN MOR
(From page 65)

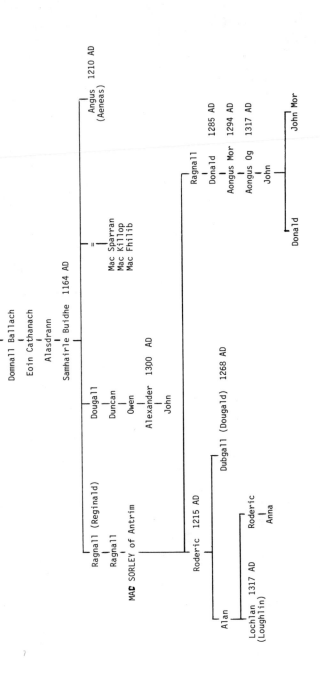

67

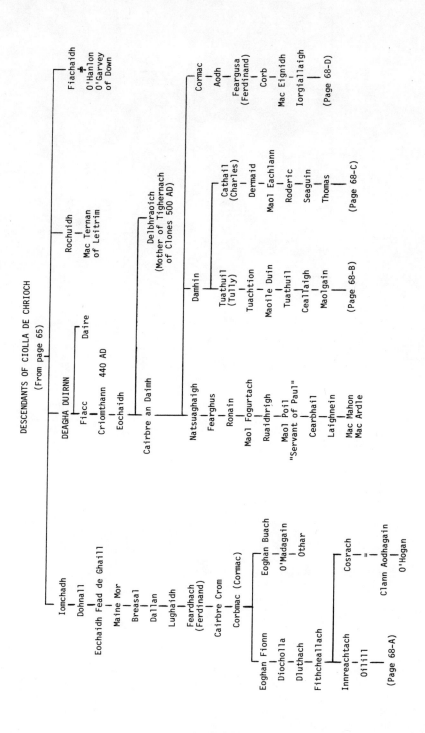

DESCENDANTS OF CIOLLA DE CHRIOCH
(From page 65)

68

DESCENDANTS OF CIOLLA de CHRIOCH
(From page 67)

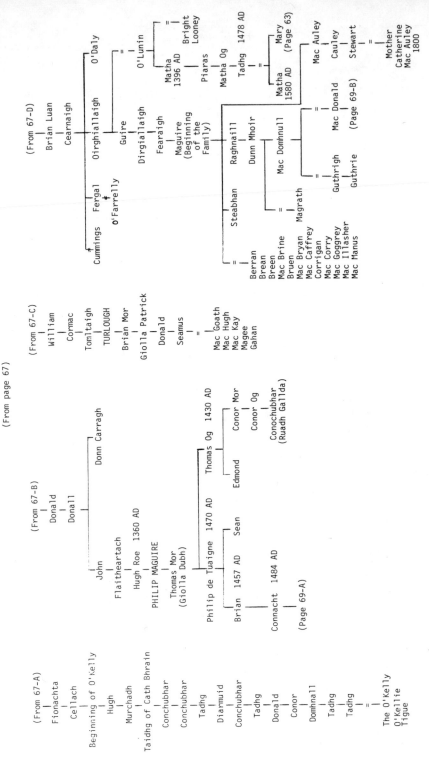

DESCENDANTS OF MAC DONALD
(From page 68-B)

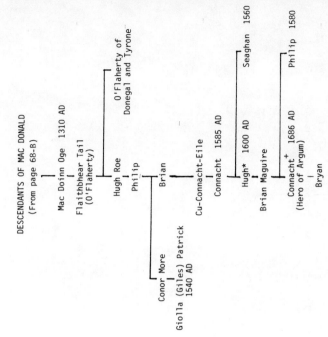

Mac Doinn Oge 1310 AD

Flaithbhear Tail
(O'Flaherty)

Hugh Roe   O'Flaherty of
Philip   Donegal and Tyrone

Conor More
Giolla (Giles) Patrick
1540 AD

Brian

Cu-Connacht-Eile

Connacht 1585 AD

Hugh* 1600 AD   Seaghan 1560

Brian Maguire

Connacht+ 1686 AD   Philip 1580
(Hero of Argum)

Bryan

* Hugh Maguire, on reconnaisance with his chief horseman,
   Niall Mor O'Duirnin (page 63) came upon the English
   leader, St. Ledger, quite by accident. Maguire rushed
   to the attack, both were wounded, both died of their
   wounds.

+ Died in battle at Aughrim. His cavalry officer O'Duirnin
   severed his head and returned it to the family burial ground
   in County Fermanagh.

DESCENDANTS OF CONNACHT
(From Page 68-A)

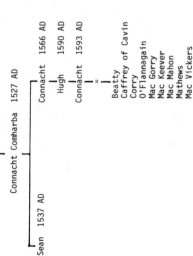

Connacht Comharba 1527 AD

Sean 1537 AD

Connacht 1566 AD

Hugh 1590 AD

Connacht 1593 AD
=
Beatty
Caffrey of Cavin
Corry
O'Flannagain
Mac Gorry
Mac Keever
Mac Mahon
Mathews
Mac Vickers

The following families are considered to be descendants
of CIOLLA DE CHRIOCH, page 65:

Boland, Colter, Mac Donnell, Mac Cormac, Cosgrove,
O'Curran, O'Danbig, O'Davin, Devin, Mac Egan, Mac Felan,
O'Flanagan, O'Garvey, Godfrey, O'Hanvy, O'Henrighty,
Mac Kenzie, Mac Kinna, Mac Kinney, Mac Knight, Knowlan,
O'Lonagan, Long, O'Lorcan, O'Maddon, O'Morna, O'Neny
O'Niellan

70

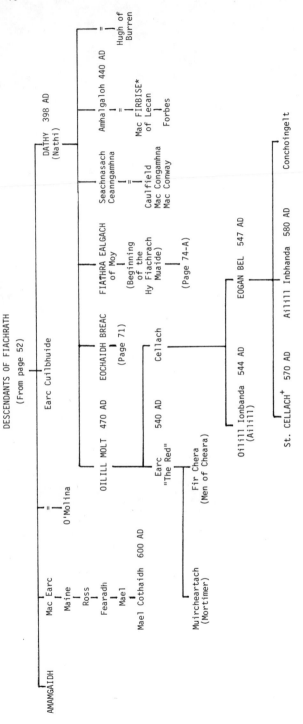

DESCENDANTS OF FIACHRATH
(From page 52)

AMAMGAIDH

Mac Earc
Maine = O'Molina
Ross
Fearadh
Mael
Mael Cothaidh 600 AD

Muircheartach
(Mortimer)

Earc Cuilbhuide

OILILL MOLT 470 AD

EOCHAIDH BREAC
(Page 71)

Earc
"The Red"
540 AD

Cellach

Fir Chera
(Men of Cheara)

DATHY 398 AD
(Nathi)

Amhalgaloh 440 AD = Hugh of Burren

Mac FIRBISE*
of Lecan
Forbes

Seachnasach
Ceanngamhna

Caulfield
Mac Congamhna
Mac Conway

FIATHRA EALGACH
of Moy

(Beginning
of the
Hy Fiachrach
Muaide)

(Page 74-A)

EOGAN BEL 547 AD

Oilill Ionbanda 544 AD
(Ailill)

St. CELLACH+ 570 AD

Ailill Inbhanda 580 AD

Conchoingelt

* Probably owner of the Book of Lecan

+ Wrote of an early history of the ancestors of the O'Conors --
Hero of the Monastary of Cluinmacnois

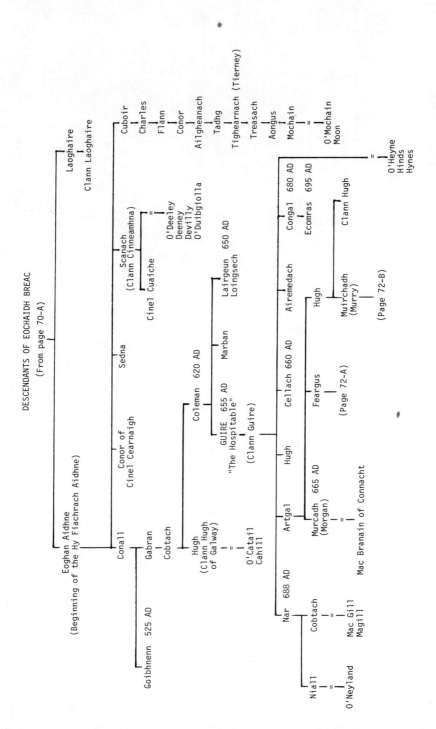

DESCENDANTS OF EOCHAIDH BREAC
(From page 70-A)

Eoghan Aidhne
(Beginning of the Hy Fiachrach Aidhne)

Laoghaire
Clann Laoghaire

Conall

Conor of Cinel Cearnaigh

Sedna

Scanach
(Clann Cinneamhna)

Cuboir
Charles
Flann
Conor
Ailgheanach
Tadhg
Tighearnach (Tierney)
Treasach
Aongus
Mochain
=
O'Mochain
Moon

Cinel Cuaiche

O'Deeley
Deeney
Devilly
O'Duibgiolla

Coleman 620 AD

GUIRE 655 AD
"The Hospitable"
(Clann Guire)

Marban

Lairgeun
Loingsech 650 AD

Goibhnenn 525 AD

Gabran
Cobtach

Hugh
(Clann Hugh
of Galway)
=
O'Catail
Cahill

Nar 688 AD

Artgal

Hugh

Cellach 660 AD

Airemedach

Congal 680 AD
Ecomras 695 AD

Clann Hugh

=
O'Heyne
Hinds
Hynes

Murcadh 665 AD
(Morgan)
=

Feargus
(Page 72-A)

Hugh

Muirchadh
(Murry)
(Page 72-B)

Mac Branain of Connacht

Niall
=
O'Neyland

Cobtach
=
Mac Gill
Magill

72

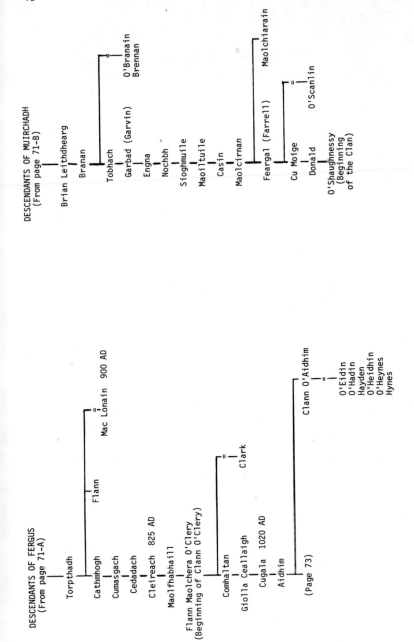

DESCENDANTS OF MUIRCHADH
(From page 71-B)

Brian Leithdhearg

Branan

Tobhach
O'Branain
Brennan

Garbad (Garvin)

Engna

Nochbh

Sioghmuile

Maoltuile

Casin

Maolcirnan

Feargal (Farrell)
Maolchiarain

Cu Moige
O'Scanlin

Donald

O'Shaughnessy
(Beginning
of the Clan)

DESCENDANTS OF FERGUS
(From page 71-A)

Torpthadh

Flann
Mac Lonain   900 AD

Cathmhogh

Cumasgach

Cedadach

Cleireach   825 AD

Maolfhabhaill

Flann Maolchera O'Clery
(Beginning of Clann O'Clery)

Comhaltan
Clark

Giolla Ceallaigh

Cugala   1020 AD

Aidhim

Clann O'Aidhim

(Page 73)

O'Eidin
O'Hadin
Hayden
O'Heidhin
O'Heynes
Hynes

DESCENDANTS OF AIDHIM
(From page 72-A)

Giolla na Naov
|
Flann
|
Conor
|
Hugh
|
Giolla (Gill)
|
Giolla of
Killikelly
(Kilelly)
Barony of Costello
Co. Mayo

In the late 1300's, Gilla-Brighde O'Clery was O'Donnell's chief historian.

O'Dhuirnin was general of O'Donnell's Horse Guard (63-88)

Families who call EOCHAIDH BREAC (page 70) their ancestor:

O'Comain, Common, Cowan, Hurly of Cork, O'Laverty, O'Lennan of Cork, Leonard, Linneen, Moran, Muldoon, O'Mulfover

The following families claim their descent from O"SHAUGHNESSY (page 72):

O'Caffy, O'Cannon, O'Cearig, O'Cemog, Creghan, O'Crocan, O'Dowda of Mayo, O'Dowel, Mac Eagin, O'Fahy, O'Keady, O;Kerin, Kieran O'Neny, Shieby

74

DESCENDANTS OF FIACHRA EALGACH
(From page 70)

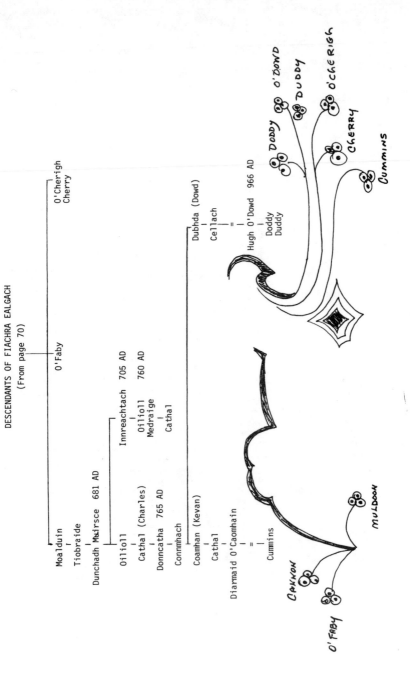

75

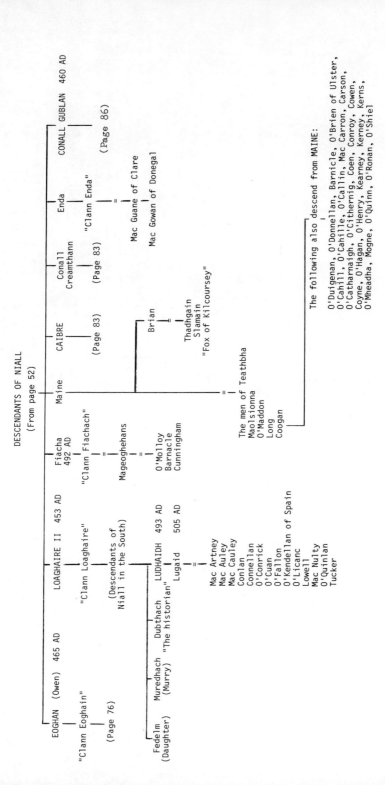

DESCENDANTS OF NIALL
(From page 52)

EOGHAN (Owen) 465 AD

"Clann Eoghain"

(Page 76)

LOAGHAIRE II 453 AD

"Clann Loaghaire"

(Descendants of
Niall in the South)

Fedelm
(Daughter)

Muredhach
(Murry)

Dubthach
"The historian"

LUDHAIDH 493 AD
Lugaid 505 AD
=

Mac Artney
Mac Auley
Mac Cauley
Conlan
Connellan
O'Conrick
O'Cuan
O'Fallon
O'Kendellan of Spain
O'Licanc
Lowell
Mac Nulty
O'Quinlan
Tucker

Fiacha
492 AD

"Clann Fiachach"

=

Mageoghehans

=

O'Molloy
Barnacle
Cunningham

Maine

=

The men of Teathbha
Maolsionna
O'Maddon
Long
Coogan

CAIBRE

(Page 83)

Brian

=

Thadhgain
Slamain
"Fox of Kilcoursey"

Conall
Creamthann

(Page 83)

Enda

"Clann Enda"

=

Mac Guane of Clare

Mac Gowan of Donegal

CONALL GUBLAN 460 AD

(Page 86)

The following also descend from MAINE:

O'Duigenan, O'Donnellan, Barnicle, O'Brien of Ulster,
O'Cahill, O'Cahille, O'Callin, Mac Carron, Carson,
O'Catharnaigh, O'Cithernig, Coen, Conroy, Cowen,
Coyne, O'Hagan, O'Henry, Kearney, Kerney, Kerns,
O'Mheadha, Mogne, O'Quinn, O'Ronan, O'Shiel

76

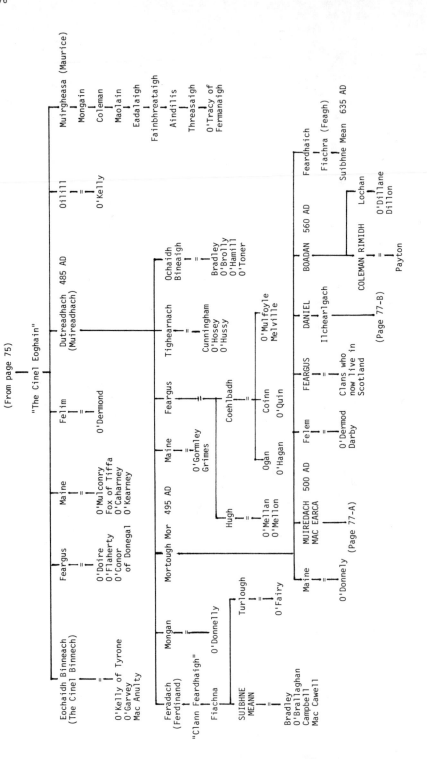

DESCENDANTS OF EOGHAN, SON OF NIALL
(From page 75)

"The Cinel Eoghain"

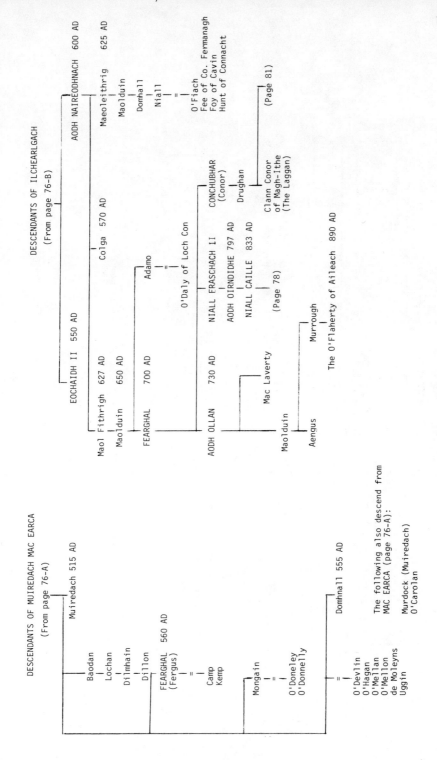

78

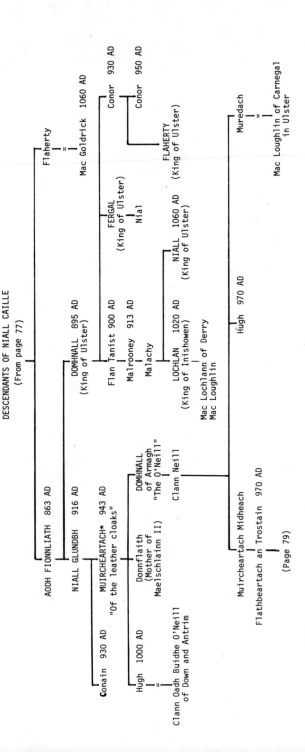

DESCENDANTS OF NIALL CAILLE
(From page 77)

Flaherty
=
Mac Goldrick 1060 AD

Conor 930 AD

Conor 950 AD

FLAHERTY
(King of Ulster)

AODH FIONNLIATH 863 AD

NIALL GLUNDBH 916 AD

MUIRCHEARTACH* 943 AD
"Of the leather cloaks"

DOMHNALL 895 AD
(King of Ulster)

Flan Tanist 900 AD

Malrooney 913 AD

Malachy

FERGAL
(King of Ulster)

Nial

DOMHNALL
of Armagh
"The O'Neill"

Clann Neill

Donnflaith
(Mother of
Maelschlainn II)

LOCHLAN 1020 AD
(King of Inishowen)

NIALL 1060 AD
(King of Ulster)

Mac Lochlann of Derry
Mac Loughlin

Muredach
=
Mac Loughlin of Carnegal
in Ulster

Hugh 970 AD

Conain 930 AD

Hugh 1000 AD
=
Clann Oadh Buidhe O'Neill
of Down and Antrim

Muircheartach Midheach

Flathbeartach an Trostain 970 AD

(Page 79)

* Inventor of the fur-lined sleeping bag.

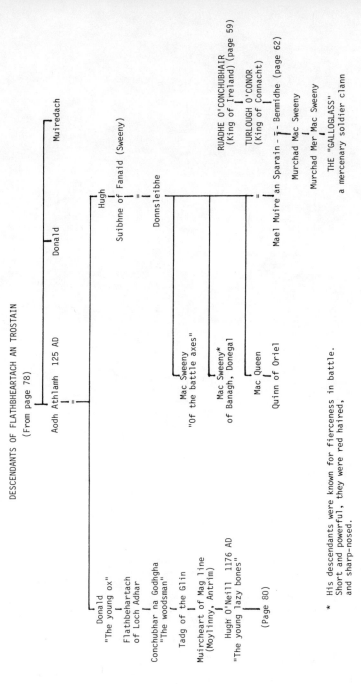

DESCENDANTS OF FLATHBHEARTACH AN TROSTAIN
(From page 78)

Muiredach

Donald

Hugh

Suibhne of Fanaid (Sweeny)

Donnsleibhe

Aodh Athlamh 125 AD
=

Mac Sweeny
"Of the battle axes"

Mac Sweeny*
of Banagh, Donegal

Mac Queen

Quinn of Oriel

Donald
"The young ox"

Flathbhartach
of Loch Adhar

Conchubhar na Godhgha
"The woodsman"

Tadg of the Glin

Muircheart of Mag line
(Moylinny, Antrim)

Hugh O'Neill 1176 AD
"The young lazy bones"

(Page 80)

RUADHE O'CONCHUBHAIR
(King of Ireland) (page 59)

TURLOUGH O'CONOR
(King of Connacht)

Mael Muire an Sparain - = - Benmidhe (page 62)

Murchad Mac Sweeny

Murchad Mer Mac Sweeny

THE "GALLOGLASS"
a mercenary soldier clann

* His descendants were known for fierceness in battle.
  Short and powerful, they were red haired,
  and sharp-nosed.

Another Mac Sweeny clann descends from Swaine, King of Norway.

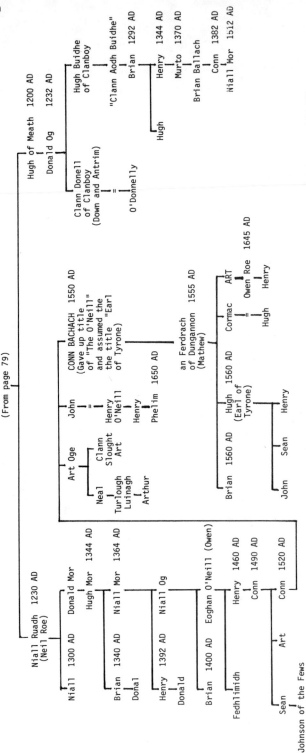

80

DESCENDANTS OF HUGH "LAZY BONES"
(From page 79)

Also descended from the O'Neills:

Mac Barron of Donegal,
Avery of Down,
O'Mellan, O'Mullan,
Mac Shane of Louth, Gilmartin

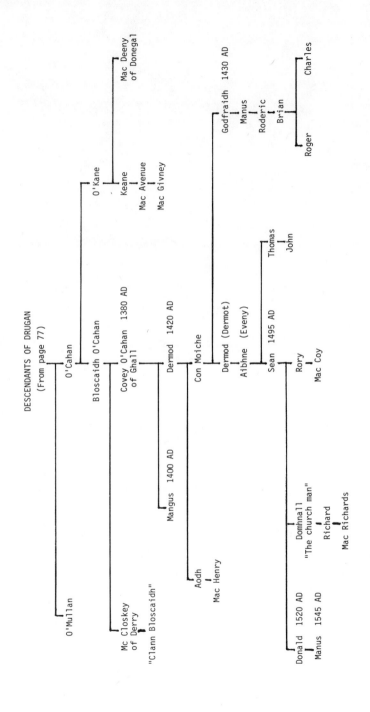

DESCENDANTS OF DRUGAN
(From page 77)

The following families claim descendancy from EOGAN, son of Niall Naoighiallach (page 75):

O'Breslin, Caolfield, Mac Caroon, O'Cathvil, Conlan, Corrigan, O'Craoibhe, O'Creagh, Donnelly, O'Donnoly, O'Duan, O'Dunegan, Dunneen, Feeney, O'Fogarty, Gorman, O'Gormly, Grimes, Mac Guirk, O'Hamilly, O'Hay, Hayes, O'Heasy, O'Hegerty, O'Horan, O'Horin, Horton, O'Kean, Mac Loughlin, O'Maolbreassal, Mitchell, O'Molloy, Mullineux, Mulville, O'Murcha, Murchie, Murchison, Shields, Mac Theobald, O'Tracy of Galway

LUÍ NA GRÉINE

"CLONMACNOISE" County - Offaly

"ANCIENT CROSS - GLENCOLUMBKILLE" County - Donegal

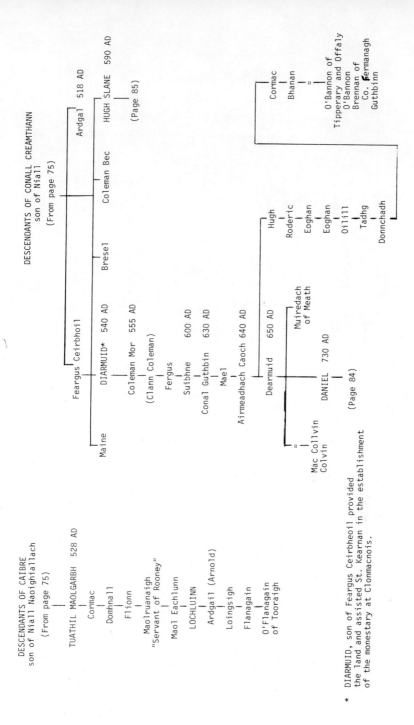

DESCENDANTS OF CONALL CREAMTHANN
son of Niall
(From page 75)

DESCENDANTS OF CAIBRE
son of Niall Naoighiallach
(From page 75)

DESCENDANTS OF CAIBRE
son of Niall Naoighiallach
(From page 75)

TUATHIL MAOLGARBH   528 AD

Cormac

Domhnall

Flionn

Maolruanaigh
"Servant of Rooney"

Maol Eachlunn

LOCHLUINN

Ardgail (Arnold)

Loingsigh

Flanagain

O'Flanagain
of Tooraigh

Maine

Feargus Ceirbhoil

Ardgal   518 AD

Coleman Bec

Bresel

DIARMUID*   540 AD

Coleman Mor   555 AD
(Clann Coleman)

Fergus

Suibhne   600 AD

Conal Guthbin   630 AD

Mael

Airmeadhach Caoch 640 AD

Dearmuid   650 AD

Muiredach
of Meath

DANIEL   730 AD
(Page 84)

Mac Collvin
Colvin
=

HUGH SLANE   590 AD
(Page 85)

Cormac

Bhanan
=

O'Bannon of
Tipperary and Offaly
O'Bannon
Brennan of
Co. Fermanagh
Guthbinn

Hugh

Roderic

Eoghan

Eoghan

Oilill

Tadhg

Donnchadh

* DIARMUID, son of Feargus Ceirbheoil provided
the land and assisted St. Kearnan in the establishment
of the monestary at Clonmacnois.

84

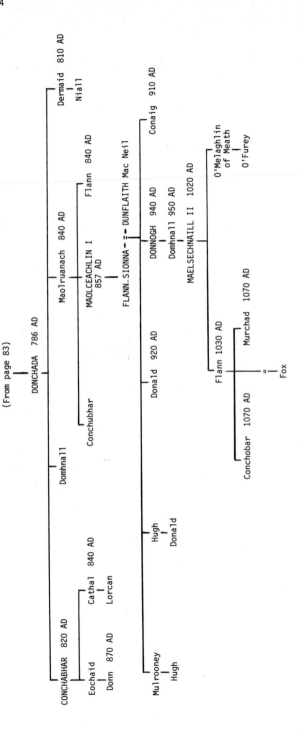

DESCENDANTS OF DANIEL
(From page 83)

DONCHADA 786 AD

CONCHABHAR 820 AD

Eochaid
Donn 870 AD

Cathal 840 AD
Lorcan

Domhnall

Maolruanach 840 AD

Conchubhar

MAOLCEACHLIN I
857 AD

Flann 840 AD

FLANN_SIONNA — = — DUNFLAITH Mac Neil

Donald 920 AD

Hugh
Donald

Mulrooney
Hugh

DONNOGH 940 AD
Domhnall 950 AD

Conaig 910 AD

MAELSECHNAILL II 1020 AD

Flann 1030 AD

Murchad 1070 AD

= — Fox

Conchobar 1070 AD

O'Melaghlin
of Meath

O'Furey

Dermaid 810 AD
Niall

DESCENDANTS OF HUGH SLANE
(From page 83)

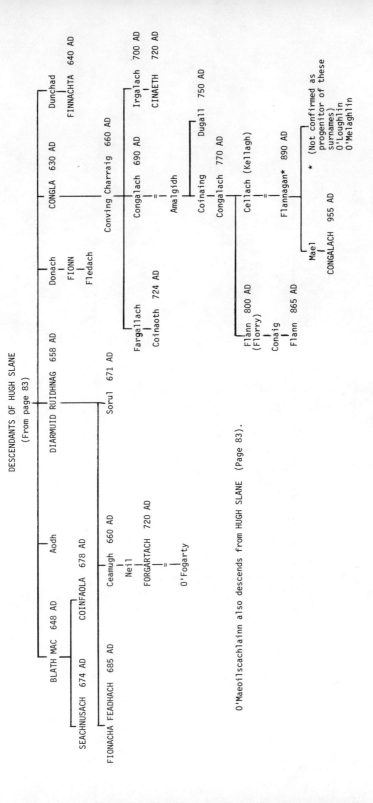

O'Maeoilscachlainn also descends from HUGH SLANE (Page 83).

86

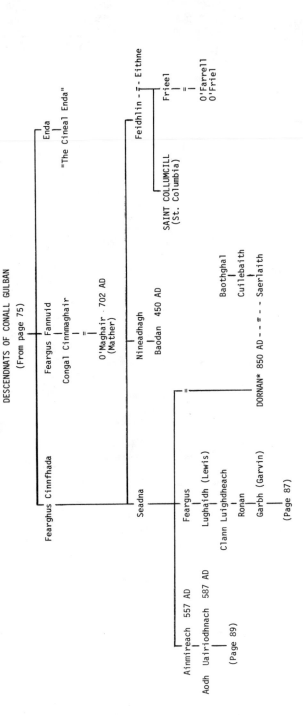

DESCENDNATS OF CONALL GULBAN
(From page 75)

Fearghus Cinnfhada

Fearghus Fannuid   Enda
Congal Cinnmaghair   "The Cineal Enda"

O'Maghair 702 AD
(Mather)

Feidhlin - ₸ - Eithne

SAINT COLUMCILL   Frieel
(St. Columbia)
                          ═
                         O'Farrell
                         O'Frieel

Nineadhagh
Baodan 450 AD

Baothghal
Cuilebaith
Saerlaith

Seadna   DORNAN* 850 AD ─ ─ ═ ─ ─

Feargus
Lughaidh (Lewis)
Clann Luighdheach
Ronan
Garbh (Garvin)
(Page 87)

Ainmireach 557 AD
Aodh Uairiodhnach 587 AD
(Page 89)

* Said to be the original owner of the illuminated manuscript
   of Mac Durnan now in the library at Lambeth palace - London

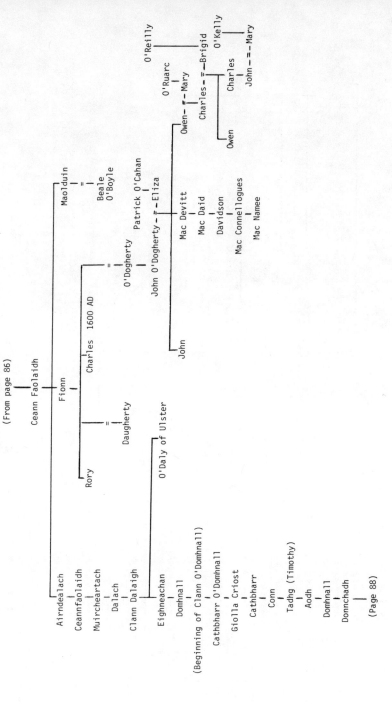

DESCENDANTS OF GARBH
(From page 86)

Ceann Faolaidh

Airndealach
Ceannfaolaidh
Muircheartach
Dalach
Clann Dalaigh

Fionn

Rory

Charles 1600 AD

Maolduin
=
Beale O'Boyle

Daugherty
=

O'Dogherty
Patrick O'Cahan

John O'Dogherty = Eliza

John

Mac Devitt
Mac Daid
Davidson
Mac Connellogues
Mac Namee

O'Reilly

O'Ruarc
Owen = Mary

Charles = Brigid
O'Kelly

Owen

Charles
John = Mary

O'Daly of Ulster

Eighneachan
Domhnall
(Beginning of Clann O'Domhnall)
Cathbharr O'Domhnall
Giolla Criost
Cathbharr
Conn
Tadhg (Timothy)
Aodh
Domhnall
Donnchadh

(Page 88)

88

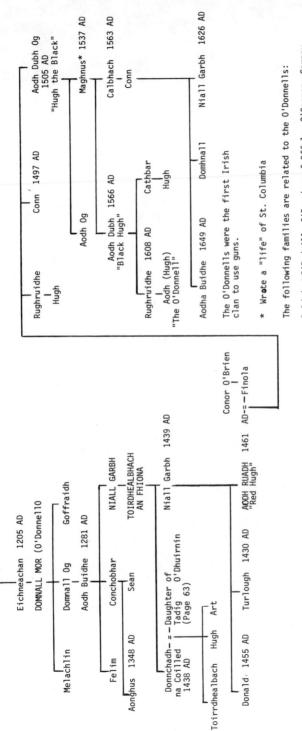

DESCENDANTS OF DONNCHADH
(From page 87)

Eichneachan 1205 AD
DONNALL MOR (O'Donnell)

Melachlin   Domnall Og   Goffraidh
              Aodh Buidhe 1281 AD

Felim   Conchobhar   NIALL GARBH
          Sean   TOIRDHEALBHACH AN FHIONA

Aonghus 1348 AD   Niall Garbh 1439 AD

Donnchadh--=--Daughter of
na Coilled   Tadig O'Dhuirnin
1438 AD   (Page 63)

Toirrdhealbach Hugh Art

Donald 1455 AD   Turlough 1430 AD   AODH RUADH 1461 AD-=-Finola
                                        "Red Hugh"   Conor O'Brien

Rughruidhe   Conn 1497 AD   Aodh Dubh Og 1505 AD "Hugh the Black"
Hugh
               Aodh Og   Maghnus* 1537 AD
                           Calbhach 1563 AD
               Aodh Dubh 1566 AD   Conn
               "Black Hugh"
                                     Cathbar
               Rughruidhe 1608 AD   Hugh
               Aodh (Hugh)
               "The O'Donnell"

Aodha Buidhe 1649 AD   Domhnall   Niall Garbh 1626 AD

The O'Donnells were the first Irish
clan to use guns.

* Wrote a "life" of St. Columbia

The following families are related to the O'Donnells:

Baldwin, O'Badgill, O'Bracken of Offaly, O'Cannon, Carney,
Mac Colivin, Clann Dala, O'Dallaghan, Deane, Diamond,
O'Hea, Kearney, Mac Lons, O'Maolmony, O'Mulligan, Mac Nerlin

DESCENDANTS OF AODH UAIRIODHNACH
(From page 86)

MAOLOCHBA 620 AD

Maolfithbh

Daniel 648 AD
Angus
Longseach 693 AD
Flaithbhlathaigh 731 AD
(Flaherty)

= Leonard

= O'Mulderry

Maolduin
Feargall Cionhmaghair 719 AD
Nialfreasach 786 AD
Hugh 837 AD

Canalclaon
Longseach
Flaithbheartagh
(Flaherty)

CELLACH 650 AD
Donall
Donncha (Dennis)
Rurai (Rory)
Ruarcan
Gallochobhair
=
O'Galligher

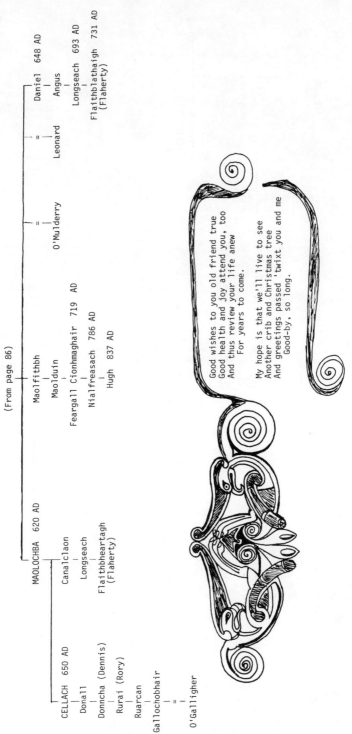

Good wishes to you old friend true
Good health and joy attend you, too
And thus review your life anew
    For years to come.

My hope is that we'll live to see
Another crib and Christmas tree
And greetings passed 'twixt you and me
    Good-by, so long.

90

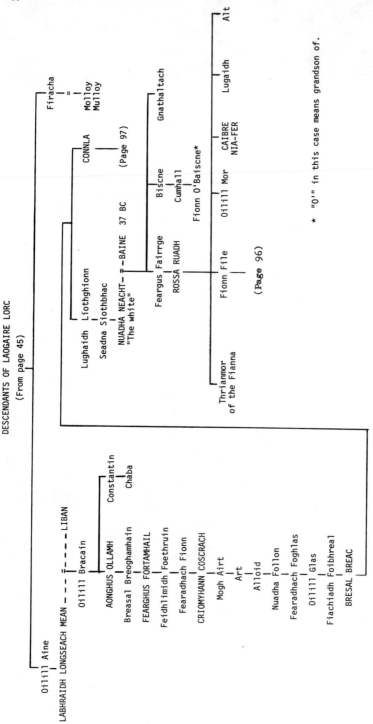

DESCENDANTS OF LAOGAIRE LORC

(From page 45)

* "O" in this case means grandson of.

DESCENDANTS OF FIONN FILE
(From page 90)

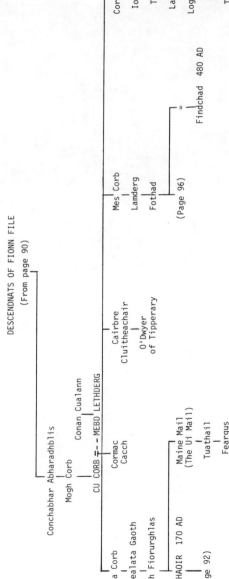
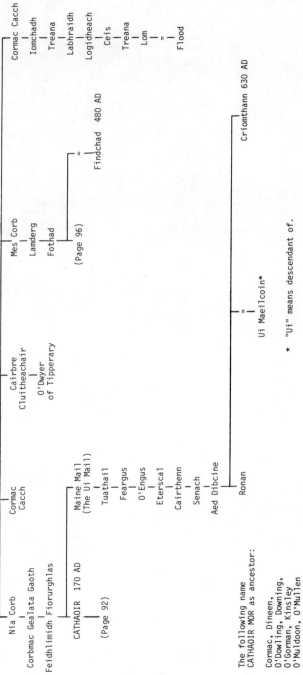

Conchabhar Abharadhblis

Mogh Corb

Conan Cualann

CU CORB = = MEBD LETHDERG

Nia Corb

Cormbac Gealata Gaoth

Feidhlimidh Fiorurghlas

Cormac Cacch

CATHAOIR 170 AD

(Page 92)

Cairbre
Cluitheachair

O'Dwyer
of Tipperary

Mes Corb

Lamderg

Fothad

(Page 96)

= =

Findchad 480 AD

Cormac Cacch

Iomchadh

Treana

Labhraidh

Logidheach

Ceis

Treana

Lom

= =

Flood

Maine Mail
(The Ui Mail)

Tuathail

Feargus

O'Engus

Eterscal

Cairthenn

Senach

Aed Dibcine

Ronan

= =

Ui Maeilcoin*

Criomthann 630 AD

* "Ui" means descendant of.

The following name
CATHAOIR MOR as ancestor:

Cormac, Dineen,
O'Dowling, Downing,
O'Gorman, Kinsley
O'Muldoon, O'Mullen

DESCENDANTS OF CATHAOR MOR
(From page 91)

ROSSA FAILGHEACH

Maolughra

Berry
O'Beary
O'Conor Faly
O'Dempsy

DAIRE BARRACH

(The Bairrche)

Nos

Caipre

Ailill Mar

Merc Erc

Brecain

Fiacha

Fionnchadha

Bresal

Fomachaidh

Feid

Muiredach Snithe

(Page 93)

Finn

Finn

Fiotbhach

FEARGHUS DUBHEADH   525 AD
"The black tooth"

Aongus Fionn

Lughaidh

Dubthaig

Dullain

Feargna

Muireheadh Munderg

Caireall
(The reincarnated)

In his previous life he was
Tuan, son of Stern (page 4)

EOCHAIDH GUNAIT* 254 AD

* The following family names come from this king:

O'Branain, O'Bresal, O'Breslin, Clann Carbry
Mac Colgaine, O'Floinus, O'Mulkieran

The following families are descendants of
DAIRE BARRACH:

O'Brenen of Ulster, O'Comane, O'Feall,
O'Follachty, Mac Gorman of Leix, O'Gorman,
O'Guban, Mallon, O'Mallone, Manning,
O'Melain, Mellon, O'Minchan, O'Mollane,
Mooney, Moynihan, Muldoon, O'Tracey of Leix,
Tracy, Smith

The following families
claim ancestorship;

Allian
O'Colgan
O;Cullen
Dindon
Mac Donagh
O 'Dondon
O'Dugan
Duffie
Duffy
O'Dun
Ennis
O'Finn
Foran
O'Foranan
O'Hart
Hartagan
O;Hennessy
O;Hoolahan
Mac Lean
Leonard
O;Maine
Morgan
Mulkieran
N olan
O'Ragan

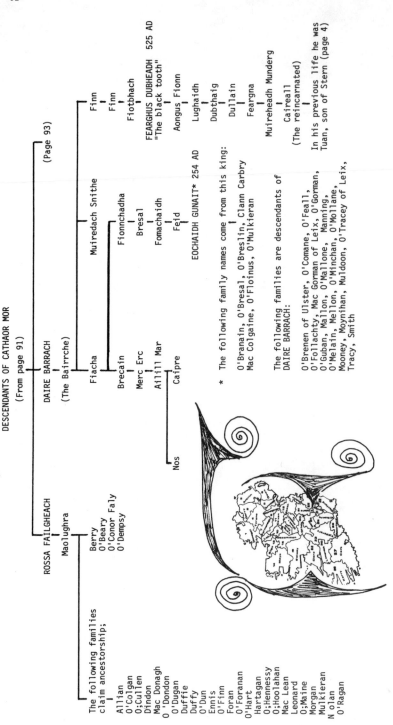

DESCENDNATS OF CATHAOIR MOR (Continued)
(From page 92)

This Clann is co-mingled
with the people of Rossa
Failgheach and in the absence
of written records cannot be
easily separated.

Criomthan of Linster

Feargus Luscan
=
Clifford
Coleman
O'Duban
Duggan
O'Ena
Gaynor
O'Geran
Mac Ginty
Mac Ginver
Mac Kenna
Killian
Kirby
Knowlan
Lacken
O'Loscan
O'Nowlan
O'Singin
O'Tilly of Co. Fermanagh

Aonghus

Fiachaidh Aiceadha
BREASAL BEALACH

Labhraidh Laidech   Eanna Niadh

(Page 94)

Toland of Mayo

O'Togill of Derry

Dunlaing

Ailill 250 AD
=
Cormac 520 AD
Coirpre
Coleman Mor 576 AD
Faelan 665 AD   O'Farrell   Ronan 620 AD

Brian Lethderg
=
O'Byrne
Burns
Hayden

Tully
Tilly

=
O'Tughill

O'Toole

Murtough O'Toole
Lord of Murresk
Co. Mayo

St. Laurence O'Toole*
Archbishop of Dublin
1170 AD

Diarmuid Mac Morrough ─ ─ Mor
(Page 94)

Earl Strong Bow ─ = ─ Eva
(See page 94, 105, 114)

Also of this line

O'Donoghue of Dublin, Ui Dunchada
(Donajoe), Ui Maeltuile (Tully), Ui
Mainchin (O'Monahan, Monks), Ui
Muiredaigh (Mac Murray, Gilmore),
O'Murry of South Kildare, Ui Nemri
(Emory?), O'Phelan (Whelan).

* Inian O'Byrne was the mother
of St. Laurence O'Toole.

Breassal Enachlas
=
O'Cuning
O'Cruchta
O'Dicolo
O'Eogan
O'Feardig

Gryffin

Eochaidh Timine
=
O'Birne
O'Copling
Hanrahan

Oilill Ceatach ?

O'Fallon of Wicklow

Deremasach
=
O'Cooney; O'Conin, O'Cuanda,
O'Deremasach, Kenyon, O'Uica

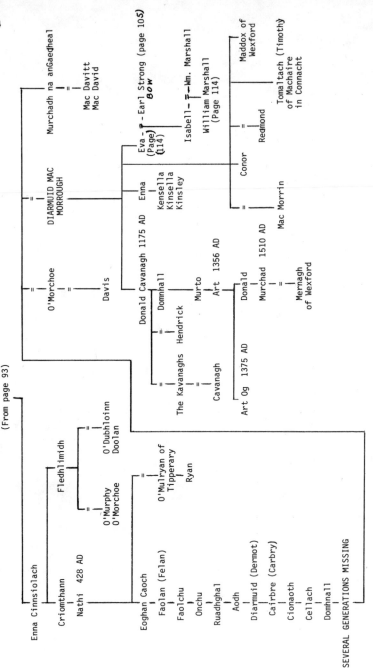

DESCENDANTS OF LABHRAIDH LAIDECH
(From page 93)

(From page 93)

94

Enna Cinnsiolach

Criomthann

Nathi 428 AD

Fledhlimidh

O'Dubhloinn
Doolan

O'Murphy
O'Morchoe

O'Mulryan of
Tipperary

Ryan

Eoghan Caoch

Faolan (Felan)

Faolchu

Onchu

Ruadhghal

Aodh

Diarmuid (Dermot)

Cairbre (Carbry)

Cionaoth

Cellach

Domhnall

SEVERAL GENERATIONS MISSING

Murchadh na anGaedheal

Mac Davitt
Mac David

DIARMUID MAC
MORROUGH

O'Morchoe

Davis

Donald Cavanagh 1175 AD

Domhnall

Hendrick

The Kavanaghs

Murto

Cavanagh

Art 1356 AD

Art Og 1375 AD

Donald

Murchad 1510 AD

Mernagh
of Wexford

Mac Morrin

Enna

Kensella
Kinsella
Kinsley

Conor

Redmond

Eva — Earl Strong (page 105)
(Page)
(114)   BOW

Isabell — Wm. Marshall

William Marshall
(Page 114)

Maddox of
Wexford

Tomaltach (Timothy)
of Machaire
in Connacht

DESCENDANTS OF FOTHAD

(From page 91)

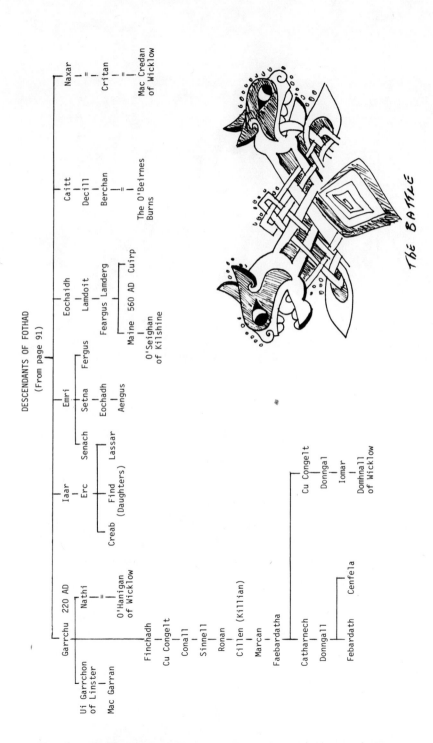

- Garrchu 220 AD
  - Ui Garrchon of Linster
    - Mac Garran
  - Nathi
    - =
      - O'Hanigan of Wicklow
  - Finchadh
    - Cu Congelt
      - Conall
        - Sinnell
          - Ronan
            - Cillen (Killian)
              - Marcan
                - Faebardatha
                  - Catharnech
                    - Donngall
                      - Febardath
                      - Cenfela
                  - Cu Congelt
                    - Donngal
                      - Iomar
                        - Domhnall of Wicklow
- Iaar
  - Erc
    - Creab
    - Find (Daughters)
    - Lassar
- Emri
  - Senach
  - Setna
    - Eochadh
      - Aengus
  - Fergus
- Eochaidh
  - Lamdoit
    - Feargus Lamderg
      - Maine
        - O'Seighan of Kilshine
      - 560 AD
      - Cuirp
- Caitt
  - Decill
    - Berchan
      - =
        - The O'Beirnes Burns
- Naxar
  - =
    - Critan
      - =
        - Mac Credan of Wicklow

THE BATTLE

DESCENDANTS OF CONNLA
(From page 90)

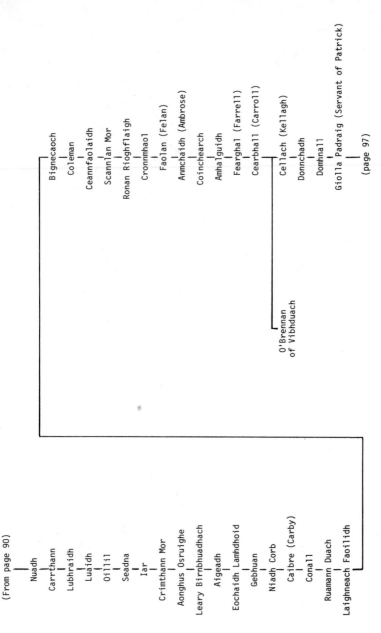

Nuadh
Carrthann
Lubhraidh
Luaidh
Oillil
Seadna
Iar
Crimthann Mor
Aonghus Osruighe
Leary Birmbhuadhach
Aigeadh
Eochaidh Lamhdhoid
Gebhuan
Niadh Corb
Caibre (Carby)
Conall
Ruamann Duach
Laighneach Faoilidh

Bignecaoch
Coleman
Ceannfaolaidh
Scannlan Mor
Ronan Rioghflaigh
Cronnmhaol
Faolan (Felan)
Anmchaidh (Ambrose)
Coinchearch
Amhalguidh
Fearghal (Farrell)
Cearbhall (Carroll)
Cellach (Kellagh)
Donnchadh
Domhnall
Giolla Padraig (Servant of Patrick)

O'Brennan
of Vibhduach

(page 97)

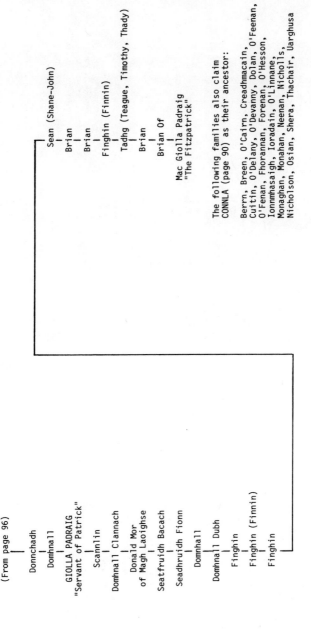

DESCENDNATS OF GIOLLA PADRAIG

(From page 96)

Donnchadh

Domhnall

GIOLLA PADRAIG
"Servant of Patrick"

Scamlin

Domhnall Clannach

Donald Mor
of Magh Laoighse

Seatfruidh Bacach

Seadhruidh Fionn

Domhnall

Domhnall Dubh

Finghin

Finghin (Finnin)

Finghin

Sean (Shane-John)

Brian

Brian

Finghin (Finnin)

Tadhg (Teague, Timothy, Thady)

Brian

Brian Of

Mac Giolla Padraig
"The Fitzpatrick"

The following families also claim
CONNLA (page 90) as their ancestor:

Berrn, Breen, O'Cairn, Creadhmacain,
Cuitin, O'Delany, O'Devanny, Dolan, O'Feenan,
O'Fenan, Fhorannan, Forenan, O'Hesson,
Ionmhasaigh, Ioradain, O'Linnane,
Monaghan, Monahan, Neenan, Nicholls,
Nicholson, Osian, Shera, Thachair, Uarghusa

98

FROM PAGE 23 - AA, BB, CC, DD, EE

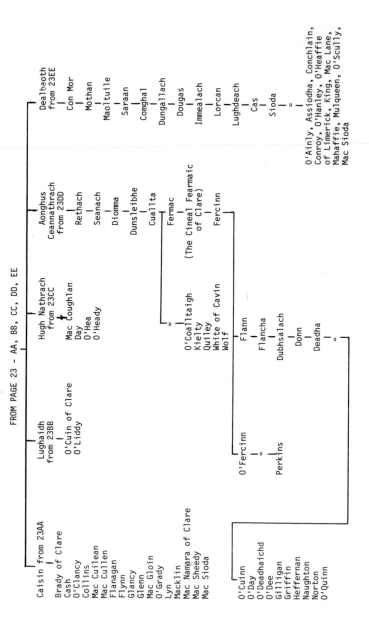

In the late 700's AD, a military breakthrough occurred in the North, probably around the present site of Bergen, Norway, which changed the fortunes of the Irish and very large areas of Europe proper. A brilliant ship builder among the people whom we call the Vikings designed a ship light in weight and yet capable of withstanding the stormy seas of the North Atlantic. About this same time, a great upheaval occurred among the population, some of whom took to their boats heading South. Ancestors of these people had visited the South many years before and some think that they were the Fomorians and the Tuatha de Dannan who are documented in Ireland's ancient Oral History. Raiding Ireland about 795, they found unexpected booty. Ireland had become a land of immense riches, much of it housed in monasteries and for all practical purposes undefended. The wealth of Ireland made expansion of the Viking raids desirable and possible. Eventually, they travelled over most of Europe, and in time founded centers of trade and settled down in such diverse places as Russia, France and Ireland. Most of the descendants of the Irish owe some portion of their inheritance to this vigorous and aggressive people.

Viking Oral History does not clearly separate "gods" from men, so for our purposes here I shall treat the "gods" as human ancestors. According to tradition, Odin (Woden) and his son Balder led their tribe from the site of Troy in Asia Minor across Europe to present day Denmark. A fragmentary geneology of this tribe is shown below:

Date of the migration to Denmark is uncertain. Some oralists think it may have been as late as the 600's AD. Others think 1600 BC.

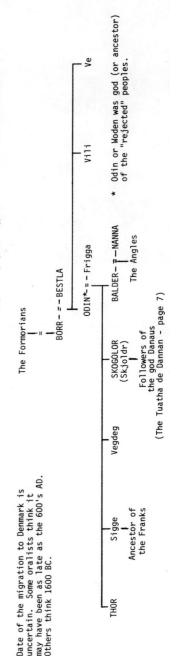

EARLY VIKINGS WHO FIGURE IN IRISH HISTORY

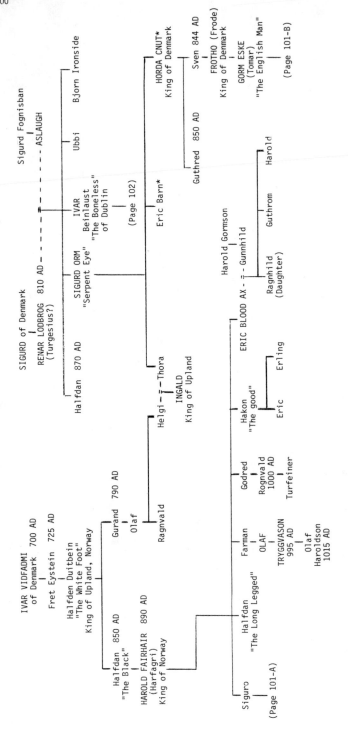

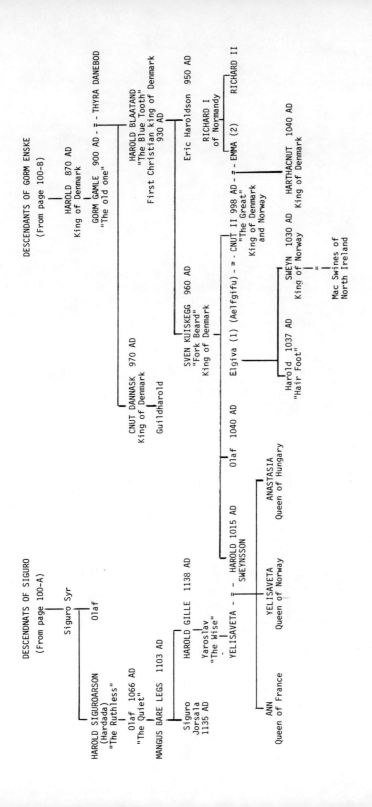

DESCENDANTS OF GORM ENSKE
(From page 100-B)

HAROLD 870 AD
King of Denmark

GORM GAMLE 900 AD - = - THYRA DANEBOD
"The old one"

HAROLD BLAATAND
"The Blue Tooth"
First Christian king of Denmark
930 AD

Eric Haroldson 950 AD

RICHARD I
of Normandy

RICHARD II

CNUT DANNASK 970 AD
King of Denmark

Guildharold

SVEN KUISKEGG 960 AD
"Fork Beard"
King of Denmark

Elgiva (1) (Aelfgifu) - = - CNUT II 998 AD - = - EMMA (2)
"The Great"
King of Denmark
and Norway

SWEYN 1030 AD
King of Norway

HARTHACNUT 1040 AD
King of Denmark

Harold 1037 AD
"Hair Foot"

Mac Swines of
North Ireland

Olaf 1040 AD

DESCENDNATS OF SIGURO
(From page 100-A)

Siguro Syr

Olaf

HAROLD SIGUROARSON
(Hardada)
"The Ruthless"

Olaf 1066 AD
"The Quiet"

MANGUS BARE LEGS 1103 AD

Siguro
Jorsala
1135 AD

HAROLD GILLE 1138 AD

Yaroslav
"The Wise"

YELISAVETA - = - HAROLD 1015 AD
SWEYNSSON

ANASTASIA
Queen of Hungary

YELISAVETA
Queen of Norway

ANN
Queen of France

102

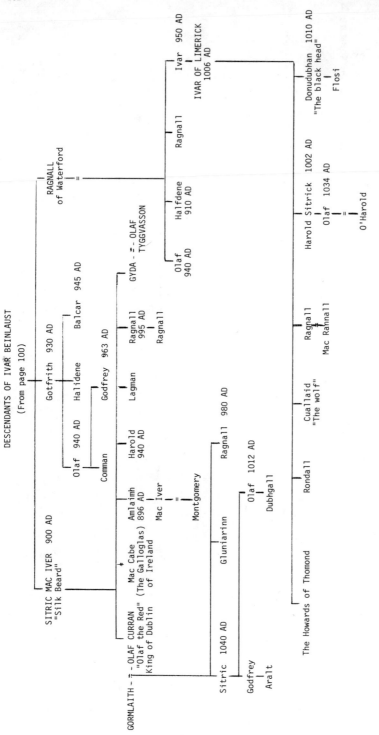

DESCENDANTS OF IVAR BEINLAUST
(From page 100)

VIKING JOINS IRISH

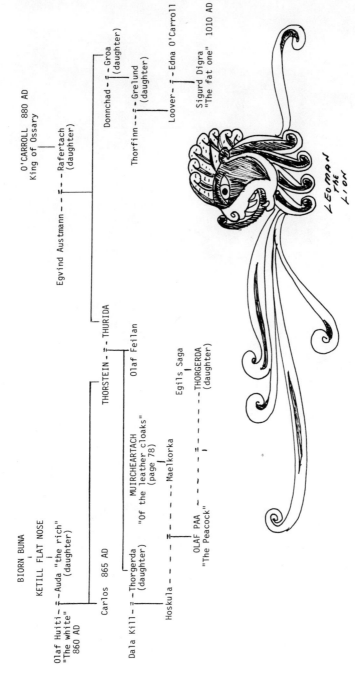

BIORN BUNA
|
KETILL FLAT NOSE

O'CARROLL 880 AD
King of Ossary

Olaf Huiti – Auda "the rich"
"The white" (daughter)
860 AD

Egvind Austmann – Rafertach (daughter)

Carlos 865 AD

THORSTEIN – THURIDA

Donnchad – Groa (daughter)

Dala Kill – Thorgerda (daughter)

MUIRCHEARTACH
"Of the leather cloaks"
(page 78)

Olaf Feilan

Thorfinn – Grelund (daughter)

Hoskula – Maelkorka

Egils Saga

OLAF PAA – THORGERDA (daughter)
"The Peacock"

Loover – Edna O'Carroll

Sigurd Digra
"The fat one" 1010 AD

LEOMAN THE LION

THE VIKINGS IN ICELAND AND AMERICA

The Vikings arrived in Iceland only to find the Irish already there. The Irish, loving solitude, packed and departed.

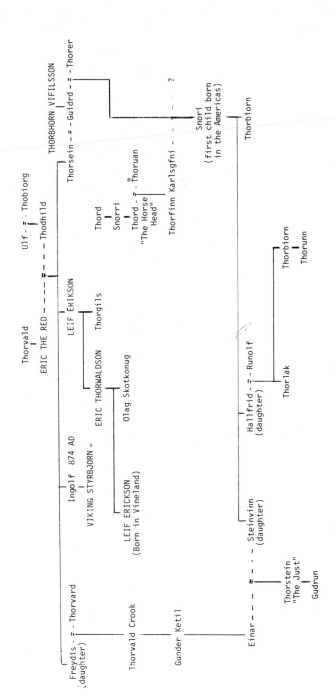

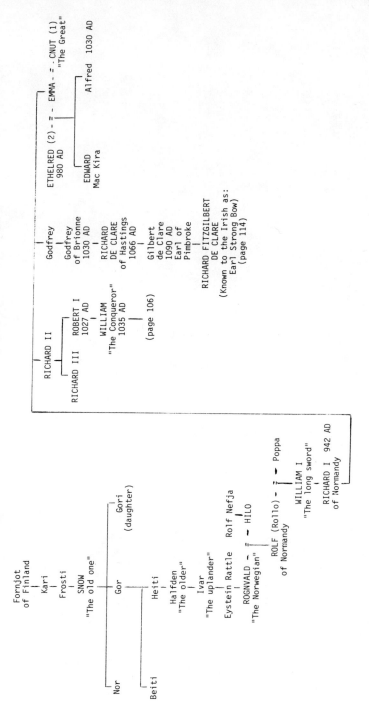

During the late 1100's, the Norman-English invaded Ireland at the request of an Irish King.

The new arrivals also considered themselves to be descendants of the Vikings.

105

Fornjot
of Finland

Kari

Frosti

SNOW
"The old one"

Gori
(daughter)

Gor

Nor

Heiti

Halfden
"The older"

Ivar
"The uplander"

Eystein Rattle   Rolf Nefja

ROGNVALD – ᛏ – HILO
"The Norwegian"

Beiti

ROLF (Rollo) – ᛏ – Poppa
of Normandy

WILLIAM I
"The long sword"

RICHARD I 942 AD
of Normandy

RICHARD II

RICHARD III   ROBERT I
               1027 AD

WILLIAM
"The Conqueror"
1035 AD

(page 106)

Godfrey

Godfrey
of Brionne
1030 AD

RICHARD
DE CLARE
of Hastings
1066 AD

Gilbert
de Clare
1090 AD
Earl of
Pimbroke

RICHARD FITZGILBERT
DE CLARE
(Known to the Irish as:
Earl Strong Bow)
(page 114)

ETHELRED (2) – ᛏ – EMMA – ᛏ – CNUT (1)
980 AD   "The Great"

EDWARD
Mac Kira

Alfred 1030 AD

106

DESCENDANTS OF WILLIAM THE CONQUORER
(From page 105)

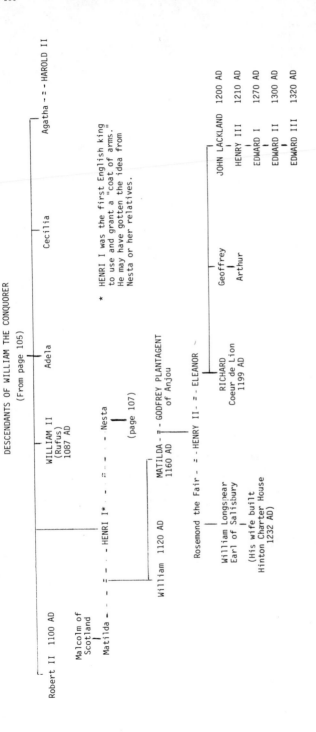

Robert II 1100 AD

Malcolm of
Scotland

Matilda - - - = - - - HENRI I* - - - :: - - - - Nesta

(page 107)

William 1120 AD   MATILDA - = - GODFREY PLANTAGENT
                    1160 AD   of Anjou

Rosemond the Fair - = - HENRY II - = - ELEANOR

William Longspear   RICHARD
Earl of Salisbury   Coeur de Lion
                           1199 AD
(His wife built
Hinton Charter House
1232 AD)

WILLIAM II   Adela   Cecilia   Agatha - = - HAROLD II
(Rufus)
1087 AD

Geoffrey   JOHN LACKLAND   1200 AD
Arthur
                  HENRY III   1210 AD

                  EDWARD I   1270 AD

                  EDWARD II   1300 AD

                  EDWARD III   1320 AD

* HENRI I was the first English king
   to use and grant a "coat of arms."
   He may have gotten the idea from
   Nesta or her relatives.

107

THE WELSH AND THE IRISH

As noted on page 105, Nesta I was the wife of HENRY I. Her natural appeals attracted other husbands and lovers and numerous descendants of these relationships became powerful invaders who shaped the future destiny of Ireland. I shall, thus, insert her genealogy before continuing with the Normans.

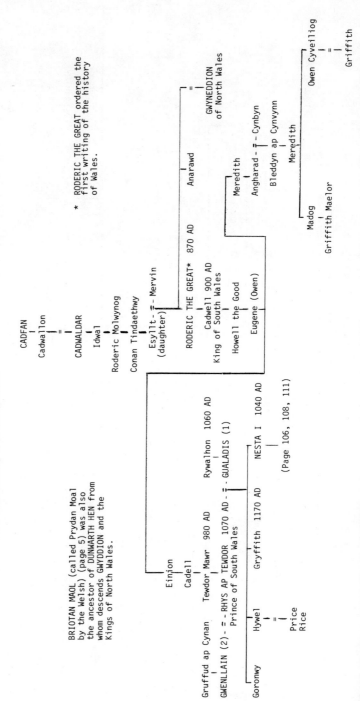

* RODERIC THE GREAT ordered the first writing of the history of Wales.

CADFAN
|
Cadwallon
=
CADWALDAR
|
Idwal
|
Roderic Molwynog
|
Conan Tindaethwy
|
Esyllt - ╤ - Mervin
(daughter)
|
RODERIC THE GREAT*   870 AD
|
Cadwell   900 AD
King of South Wales
|
Howell the Good
|
Eugene (Owen)

Anarawd
|
GWYNEDDION
of North Wales

Meredith
|
Angharad - ╤ - Cynbyn
Bleddyn ap Cynvynn
|
Meredith
|
Madog
|
Griffith Maelor

Owen Cyveiliog
=
Griffith

BRIOTAN MAOL (called Prydan Moal by the Welsh) (page 5) was also the ancestor of DUNWARTH HEN from whom descends GWYDDION and the Kings of North Wales.

Gruffud ap Cynan
|
Einjon
|
Cadell
|
Tewdor Mawr   980 AD
|
Rywalhon   1060 AD

GWENLLAIN (2) - ╤ - RHYS AP TEWDOR   1070 AD - ╤ - GUALADIS (1)
Prince of South Wales

NESTA I   1040 AD

(Page 106, 108, 111)

Goronwy
|
Hywel
=
Price
Rice

Gryffith   1170 AD

NORMAN AND WELSH ADVENTURERS DESCENDED FROM
LOPEZ OF FLORENCE

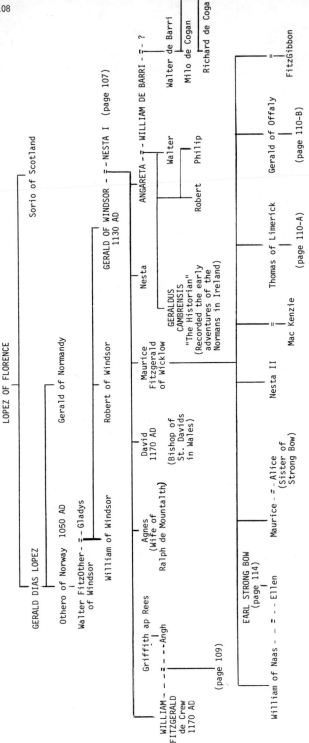

109

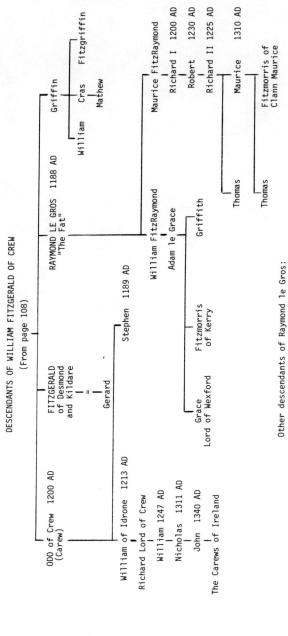

DESCENDANTS OF WILLIAM FITZGERALD OF CREW
(From page 108)

ODO of Crew 1200 AD
(Carew)

FITZGERALD
of Desmond
and Kildare
=
Gerard

RAYMOND LE GROS 1188 AD
"The Fat"

Griffin

William   Cras   Fitzgriffin
           Mathew

William of Idrone 1213 AD

Stephen 1189 AD

William FitzRaymond

Maurice FitzRaymond

Richard I 1200 AD

Robert   1230 AD

Richard II 1225 AD

Maurice   1310 AD

Richard Lord of Crew

William 1247 AD

Nicholas 1311 AD

John 1340 AD

The Carews of Ireland

Adam le Grace

Grace
Lord of Wexford

Fitzmorris
of Kerry

Griffith

Thomas

Thomas

Fitzmorris of
Clann Maurice

Other descendants of Raymond le Gros:

Carey
de Carew
Carr
Mac Elhair
Karr
O'Keary

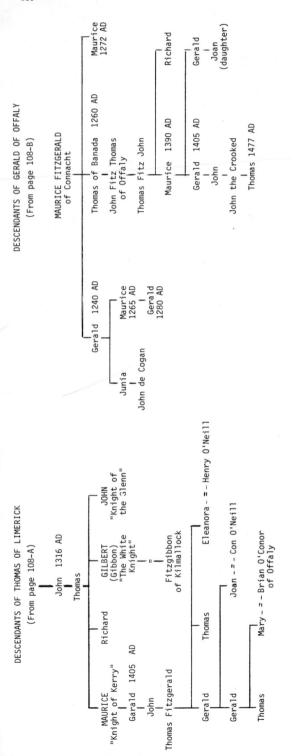

DESCENDANTS OF GERALD OF OFFALY
(From page 108-B)

MAURICE FITZGERALD
of Connacht

Gerald 1240 AD

Thomas of Banada 1260 AD

Maurice 1272 AD

Junia
John de Cogan

Maurice 1265 AD

Gerald 1280 AD

John Fitz Thomas
of Offaly

Thomas Fitz John

Maurice 1390 AD

Richard

Gerald 1405 AD

Gerald

John

Joan
(daughter)

John the Crooked

Thomas 1477 AD

DESCENDANTS OF THOMAS OF LIMERICK
(From page 108-A)

John 1316 AD

Thomas

MAURICE
"Knight of Kerry"

Richard

GILBERT
(Gibbon)
"The White
Knight"
=

JOHN
"Knight of
the Glenn"

Gerald 1405 AD

John

Thomas Fitzgerald

Fitzgibbon
of Kilmallock

Gerald

Thomas

Eleanora - = - Henry O'Neill

Gerald

Joan - = - Con O'Neill

Thomas

Mary - = - Brian O'Conor
of Offaly

The following families in Linster
descend from the Fitzgeralds:

Barron, Bodkin, Mad Edmond, Mac Fabrene,
Frazer, Mac Thomaisin, Mac Thomas,
Westley, Wellesley

DESCENDANTS OF NESTA I AND HENRY I OF ENGLAND
(From page 106)

HENRY I - = - NESTA I
|
Henry

Miler Fitz Henry   Robert Fitz Henry   Henry Fitz Henry

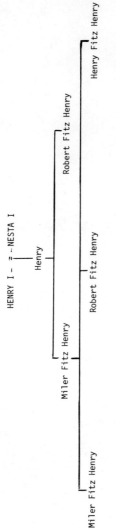

DESCENDANTS OF NESTA I AND STEPHEN OF CARDIGAN

Stephen - = - NESTA I
|
Robert Fitz Stephen   Meredith Fitz Stephen

Ralph Fitz Stephen 1188 AD
|
(daughter) - = - Milo de Cogan

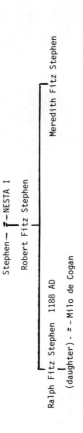

112

THE DE BURGO (BURKE) FAMILY IN IRELAND

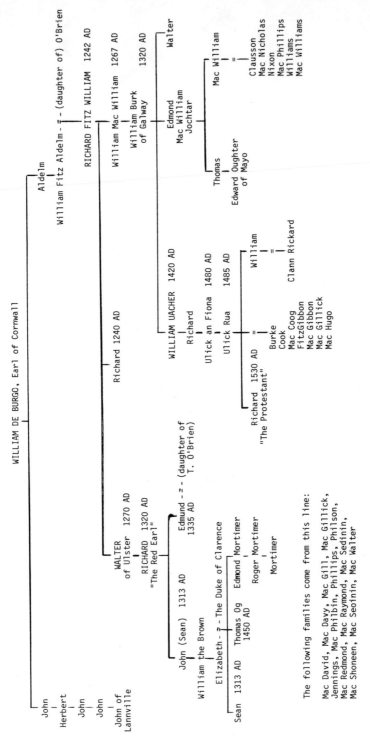

The following families come from this line:

Mac David, Mac Davy, Mac Gill, Mac Gillick,
Jennings, Mac Philbin, Phillips, Philson,
Mac Redmond, Mac Raymond, Mac Sedinin,
Mac Shoneen, Mac Seoinin, Mac Walter

113

DESCENDANTS OF LE BOTILLER (BUTLER) IN IRELAND

THEOBOLD LE BOTILLER FITZ WALTER (BUTLER)

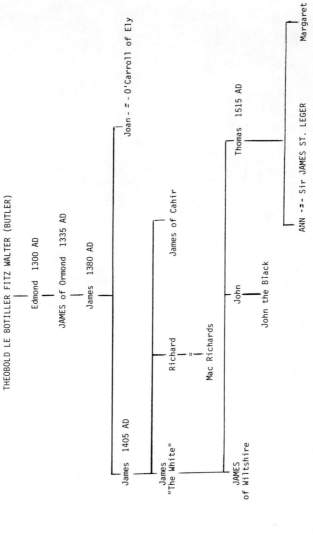

Edmond 1300 AD

JAMES of Ormond 1335 AD

James 1380 AD

Joan - = - O'Carroll of Ely

James 1405 AD

James "The White"

Richard
=
Mac Richards

James of Cahir

JAMES of Wiltshire

John

John the Black

Thomas 1515 AD

ANN - = - Sir JAMES ST. LEGER

Margaret

Some butlers changed their name to Kenton.

114

THE GENEALOGY OF EARL RICHARD FITZGILBERT DE CLARE CALLED "STRONG BOW"

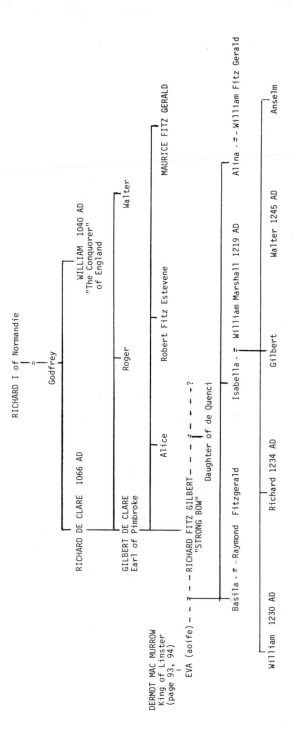

OTHER NORMAN AND WELSH INVADERS

Tradition has not retained the family names of all who came over during the early years of the Norman Invasion, however, those names listed below were very likely among the early arrivals and remained long enough to establish themselves in Irish tradition:

la Ahunty, Mac Andrew, de Angulo, Mac Aveely, Bailey, Barnes, Barrett, Barrington, Barry, Bermingham, Bird, Bissette, Blake, Bluet, de Bohun, de Braosa, Bree, Broderick, Buckley, deBurgo, Butcher, Caddell, Mac Cahey, Canteton, Cantwell, Chamberlin, Condon, Corey, Mac Corish, Crosbie, Costello, de Courcy, de Courtenay, Denny, O'Dulanty, Dullard, Edderly, Mac Evilly, Mac Feorais, Mac Ferrand, Fitzbernard, Fitzgodobert, Fitzhugh, le Fleming, de Gernemie, Gilboy, de Glanvil, Gukin, Hackett, Haney, Haskins, de Hastings, de Hay, Henry, de Hereford, O'Hiskeen, Hodnet, Howth, Howth, St. John, Mac Keon, O'Keoneen, Mac Knight, de Lacy, de St. Lawrence (changed to Howth), Mandeville, Markrell, Mac Maurice, May, de Moleyns, Mullineaux, Nagle, Nott, Mac Padden, Padine, Mac Patrick, Patterson, de Pendergast, Petty, Plunkett, le Poer (Power), Mac Quillan, de Quiney (Quincy), de Ridelsford, Mac Ruddery (Rudd?), de Rupe (Roche), de Salisbury, Savage, Mac Sherry, Mac Shoneen, Smith, Staunton, Timmons, Tyrrell, de Verdon, Waldron, Walsh . . .

As the time period with which this book deals, comes to an end, other nationalities were arriving. These included Spanish, Scotch, English, Germans and a smattering of other Europeans.

Contrary to popular belief, tourism was brisk between Ireland and the continent from as early as 100 AD, Irish raiding parties went far into Europe seeking booty and slaves. The Phonecians developed a good market for Irish products along the Mediterranean coast and there exists fair evidences that they, with Irish help, made trips to the Americas at a very early period.

During the Dark Ages, Ireland was the center of learning for all Europe. During this period many Church people visited the Holy Land. In later times, Ireland mounted an intensive missionary crusade exporting people and learning to reestablish culture in Europe.

For more than 1000 years, Ireland's chief export has been people, thus it is little wonder that so many of us are discovering that we are, at least, "a wee bit Irish."

OUR FAMILY NAMES

Prior to the year 1000 most of our ancestors had but a single name. Usually it was descriptive of a physical characteristic or a great deed. They were further identified as the "Son of -", who was the "Son of -", with two or more generations being mentioned.

A small number of families gained sufficient status for a hero ancestor's name to be firmly attached to all descendants, thus establishing one of the very early surnames.

Caoimh (Caoime) is an example. The word is descriptive and might be defined as, "The Good Looking One". It was used as a personal name as early as 900 AD. Shortly thereafter it became the surname O'Caoimh. This name translated into English is the familiar O'Keefe (Page 18). We can assume that this family exercised considerable authority due to the fact that "O'" was retained by most branches during times of political and religious persecution which induced many Irish families to "Englishize" their surname by dropping the "O'". Another indicator of their power is the fact that until very recent times they remained mostly in the single County of Cork.

I must apologize to this illustrious family, for it, like many others, is represented in this work as an appendage of an early ancestor rather than by a detailed lineage - but it is the subject of further research.

Tradition tells us that the choice of surnames by our Gaelic Ancestors differed from the method used by the Feudalistic nations. Most of our surnames related to people and were ancestral in nature. The Feudalistic nations chose surnames from "Things", such as color, work, animal, place, etc. These choices, in my opinion, serve to illustrate one difference in thinking which separated the Nomadic and Feudalistic societies.

Since the Gaelic names were ancestral, a bridge from one generation to another was devised. Ancient forms were: Ua and Ui (male and female descendants

of:). In later times "O'" became common. We would
most usually find this connector used in the sense
of, "The grandson of:" although it also meant,
"Head of the Family", or "Head of the Clan". In
the genealogies compiled in later times "Mc" served
to connect one generation to another and thus came
to mean "Son of -", which, in turn, became the pre-
fix "Mac".

Prior to the invention of type, all documents were
handwritten. With the possible exception of the
Egyptians, the Irish created some of the finest
manuscripts known. Writing, however, was a labori-
ous task and many Gaelic names required more letters
than our names today. To speed up the copying
process a form of "Shorthand" developed. Many of
the old records written in this manner can be read
only by specially trained scholars. Some writers
chose to write in Latin, others used both languages
interchangeably, employing the most expressive one
for the work they were doing. As time passed,
translation of these documents into English almost
became a lost art.

Irish Gaelic, in common with other languages,
changed with the passage of time and appears in at
least three forms; old, middle and modern Irish.
English likewise experienced at least three changes,
and to these can be added scribal errors. The result, as far as our families are concerned, was a
variety of spellings resulting in numerous family
branches, and in the case of translation, frequently
an entirely different family name.

The Index reflects many of these variations and is
valuable in itself as a study of the changes of name
forms. It should also be noted that not all names
in the index have been cross-indexed.

The older people in Ireland, particularly in the
west, still retain a keen interest in family relationships. Once the purpose of my visit became
known they expressed a warm, friendly and helpful
interest. Many exhibited a knowledge beyond expec-
tation, quoting on occasion from "The Genealogies"
of D. Mac Firbish (Dubthalthach Mac Firbhisigh).
This great historian of the west wrote during the
1600's and met an untimely death at the hands of

an assassin. Others seemed to have read Dr. James
Anderson's "Royal Genealogies of Emperors, Kings
and Princes", published in London around 1736.

A surprisingly large number of western Irish are
present representatives of the old legal, educational and poetic families. Some are fluent in
Gaelic and others have a keen memory of their traditions. Many modern Irish writers have drawn on
the memories of these talented story tellers, but
to my knowledge none have so far charted the relationships of families to these folk tale heroes.
Thus it is my hope that this book, when used in
conjunction with history and these many wonderful
stories, will help the reader to establish a
closeness to the tradition of our ancestors.

Dr. Edward MacLysaght, formally Chief Herald, and
one of Ireland's most knowledgeable genealogists,
has made numerous contributions to the art of family
research. Two of his most recent works, "Irish
Families", published by Crown of New York, and "The
Surnames of Ireland", published by the Irish
University Press of Dublin, shed much light on
family names which have not been included in this
volume.

Thus my purpose is to encourage the reader to seek
family knowledge from every source and to record
"The Doings of the Family" as a gift to future
generations. After all, the ancestors many of us
are so diligently seeking were the "Common Folk"
of earlier centuries, and we can expect that our
descendants will be as interested in us as we are
in our ancestors.

                HOW TO USE THE NAME INDEX

The index is a guide to the location of your surname
in the tables. It shows the relationship between
your English name and its traditional Gaelic form,
and is usually accompanied by a number of variations.

Your English name may stand in for one, two, or
sometimes more, original Irish family names.

After locating your surname in the index, note the
number following the English form of your surname.
This number indicates the page where your name is
to be found. Next to the page number is another
number in parentheses, ( ). This number designates
the County where persons of your surname have lived.

Now turn to the page number where your name is recorded. In some cases many names are listed together under the name of a remote ancestor. If
this should be the case with yours, this means that
your immediate traditional ancestors have not yet
been found and that persons responding knew only of
their relationship to the ancestor shown. Turn to
this particular ancestor and, using a colored pen,
trace along the connecting lines from this name to
the front of the book. Each name in capitals in
this ancestral line is an important person and can
usually be found in a good history of Ireland. Your
name and the others shown with it are the subject
of continued research.

If informants could provide a more or less complete
lineage, then your surname will be connected directly into the chart. Trace back through your
traditional ancestral line as indicated above. Most
lines have one or more generations missing. These
omissions have been indicated thusly, =, if their
absence is evident.

Now look up the Counties where your family lived and
make a note of them.

With this information at hand you are ready to visit
your library or book store (do not forget your
college or genealogical library if one is available),
to choose a good Irish history, and enjoy an inves-
tigation of your past.

This book represents, I believe, the most complete
chart of Irish family lines currently available.
Obviously many names remain to be researched, and
if I have missed yours please accept my apology.

It should be clearly understood that family lines
appearing in the charts do not guarantee a genetic
lineage for every person of your surname. Many
people, of whatever nationality, may today possess
surnames quite different from their genetic original.

A detailed study of surnames is beyond the scope of this book, but a subject I would encourage you to look into.

The average person should consider himself most fortunate if his surname can be validated for more than five generations. We Irish are more fortunate than most because of the interest our ancestors took in this subject. It is this interest which makes it possible to trace many Irish surnames to dates before 1600.

Pain and sorrow accompanied many of our ancestors in the departure from their native land. Some, with no hope of return, wiped all remembrance of Ireland from their minds and looked only to the future. Descendants of these persons are unlikely to have much knowledge of their past, and it is they whom I hope will find this book most helpful.

Obviously much work remains to be done and the society invites you to contribute data in your possession toward the end of placing on record a better view of our collective past.

All art work is the artists impression of the spirit which our ancestors sought to convey by this talent. Irish art is a study in it's own right. Ask your book dealer for information about some of the recently published works on this subject.

Note: Not all surnames shown on the charts have been indexed! Please check each chart page for hidded bits of information.

122

MORRIS

O MADDEN

DALLOWAYE

NOTE: Occasionally an English name stands in for both an Irish
and Norman family.

* Name also common in this country.

a

MAC ADAM   13   (8)
See Berry   Scotch

MAC ADAMS   48-57   (5-11)
Mac Adaim?
Mac Cadden?
Mac Caw of Cavin?
Kinnavy?

MAC AFFEE
See Mac Duffie

AGHEY?   41   (4-5-8)
Mac Eochaidh of Linster?
Mac Eachaidh
Mac Gahey of Ulster?
Oghy
Hackett?

O'AHEARN   25   (27)
O'hEachthighearna?
Ua Eichthighern?
O'Ahern
O'Ahiarn

O'AINGIDY   25

AINLY   98   (15)
O'hAinle
O' Hanley

AKIN   65   (3)
O' hOgain
O' Hagan

MAC ALARY   30   (3-13)
Mac Giolla Arraith
Mac Cleary
Clark

MAC ALIFFE   41-19   (3)
Mac Amhlaoibh   Norse
Mac Auliffe
Macafee

MAC ALLEN   13   (3)
of Britain
McCallan   (England)*

MAC ALPIN of Ulster 13 (20-23)
O' hAilin   Scotch
O' hAillin
Mac Allen
Mac Callen
O' Hallin
Hallinan

Mac ANAGLAOICH   41

MAC ANAWE   48   (2-3)
See Adams

MAC ANDREW   115   (14)
Mac Aindriu   Norman-Welsh
Barrett

de ANGULO   115
Changed name to   (14-19-27)
Nagle, later to   Norman
Costello

MAC ANULTY of   76
Meath
Mac Nulty

MAC ARDLE   67   (8-9)
Mac Ardghail
See Mac Mahon

MAC ARTAIN   39
Mac Airteain   (6-26-27)
Mac Cairteain
Mac Cartan of Down
Mac Cartain
Mac Carton

ARTHUR   21-29
Mac Arthur   (2-3-30)
Mac Carter   Norse-Scotch

MAC ARTNEY   75   (1-5)
See Mac Auley

ASSIODHA   98

MAC AULEY 68 (1-3)
Mac Amhlaimh
Mac Amhlaoidh
Mac Artney
Mac Cauley

MAC AVEELY 115
See Stanton

*AVERY of Down 80 (6)
Mac Aimhreidh

MAC AVINUE 81 (1-11)
Mac Dhuibhne
Mac Deeney
Mac Evinney
Mac Evinney

b

BADGER 41
See O'Brock

O'BADGILL 88 (20)

BAILEY 115
Bailleux (3-6-32)
Bailie
Bailey
Bayley

BAKER 65 (28)
English

BANNON 83 (20-23)
O'Banain
O'Bannan
Guthbinn

BARRETT 115
Bairead (14-19-27)
Mac Andrew

BARNES 115
See Barrington

BARNILLE
See Cowen

BARRINGTON 115 (1-22)
O'Bearain Norman
Barron
Barnes

BARRON 110
Mac Baron of Munster (27-28-32)
Frazier

MAC BARRON 80 (1-3)
O'Barun
A Branch of O'Neill

BEALE 87 (3)
Beatley
See O'Boyle

BERRY 13-92 (3-14)
O'Baire
O'Bearra
Mac Adam
A Branch of O'Dempsey

BEATLEY
See Beale

BEATTY 69
O'Biatagh (3-5-6-18)
Beatagh Danish-Irish
Beattie
Beaty
Betty

O'BEIRNE 56-57-95
See O'Birn (10-15)

BERMINGHAM 115
de Bermingham (9-18-19-21)
Mac Feorais Norman

O'BILLRIN 17

BIRD 115 (18-27)
le Oiseau Norman
Mac Aney
Mac Anneeny
Mac Eneany
Heanahan
Henry

O'BIRN 57-93
Ua Birn (10-14-15)
O'Beirne Norse-Irish
O'Bruen
Burns
Byrne

BISSETTE 115 (3)
Became: Norman
Mac Keon of Antrim

BLAKE	115	
O'Blathmhuic	(14-18-19-27)	
O'Blathmaic	Norman	
Blawick		
Blowick		
Caddell		

BLUETT	115	
Blewett	Norman	

BODKIN	10	(19)
de Boudakyn	Norse-Norman	

de BOHUN	115	
	Norman	
BOLAND	69	
O'Beollain	(21-22-25)	

O'BOLAND	25	(13-22)
O'Behellan		
O'Beolane		
O'Beollain		
O'Bowlane		

BOWEN	25	(27)
O'Cnaimhin	Welsh	
ab Owen		

O'BOYLAN	57	
Ua Baigheallain	(8-11-18)	
O'Baoighellain		
O'Boyland		

O'BOYLE	87	
Ua Baeighell	(1-3-4-5-9-14)	
O'Baethghaile		
O'Beahilly		
O'Bighell		
Beale		

O'BRAC	50	(20-21)
O'Breacain?		

O'BRACKEN	88	(20)
O'Breacain		

O'BRADIN	59	
O'Bhraoin	(3-18-23)	
Mac Brine		

BRADLEY	76	
O'Brollachain	(1-2-4-27)	
O'Brolchan		
Brallaghan		

MAC BRADY	55	(11)
Mac Bradaigh		

BRADY of Clare	98	
A branch of O'Grady	(93-11-22)	

MAC BRADY	53	(11)
Mac Bradaigh of Cavin		

O'BRALLAGHAN	76	(3)
See Bradley		

*MAC BRANAIN of	71	
Connacht	(1-11-14)	

MAC BRANNAN of	26-53	(1)
Roscommon		
See Brennan		

de BRAOSA	115	
	Norman	

BRASSILL	65	(28)
O'Breasail		
Brazell		
Brazil		

BRYE	
See Bree	

BREAN	68	(18-26)
Ua Braen		
Ua Braen		
Mac Braoin of Kilkenny		
Mac Breen		
Mac Brewne		
See Mac Bryan		

MAC BREARTY	32	(3)
See Murdock		

BREE	115	(25-27)
O'Breadhdha	Norman	
O'Bray		
O'Breagaig		
O'Breagda		
Brye		

BERRN	68-97	
Mac Bryan	(18-26-32)	
Mac Brine		

BRENNAN   24-72-83-92-96
Ui Bhreanainn   (1-7-13-
Ui Brenain   14-15-18-
O'Braonain   29-31)
O'Branain of Co. Fermanagh
O'Brennain of Vibhduach
Brannen
Brannon
Mac Brennan of Roscommon
O'Brenen of Ulster

BRESLIN   82-92   (1-7)
O' Maol Breassal
O'Breaslain
O'Brassel
O'Bresal
Breslane

BOXER
See Butcher

MAC BRIAN   26   (23-30)
Mac Bhriain

MAC BRIDE   29   (1-3-6)
Mac Giolla Brighde

BRIEN   29

O'BRIEN   26
Ua Briain   (18-27-28-32)
O'Briain   (11-32)
O'Brien of Cuanach   28
O'Brien of Ulster   75
O'Brien of Wexford   25
O'Brien of Seola   64

BRIGHT of Dublin   68   (18)
O'Luineach
Looney of Cork   (27)
O'Lunin of Fermanagh   (7)

MAC BRINE   59-68   (7-11)
O' Bhraoin of Cavin
O' Braoin

O'BROCK   41   (26-28)
O' Bruic
Bric
O'Brock
Badger`

BRODERICK   14-115
O'Bruadair of Cork
Mac Bruadair of Donegal
Brodner (1-18-19-26-27-32)
Brothers   Norse-Norman
At least four separate lines
have this name. One is a
branch of the O' Driscolls.

BRODIE   29-56   (22)
Mac Bruaidedha
O' Broduibh
Bruaideagh
Mac Brody

BROLLY   29   (22)
See Brodie

O'BROLLY   76   (2-4)
O'Brolaig

BRAWLEY
See O'Brolly

*BROSNAN   43 (26-30)
O' Brosnachain of Kerry
O'Brosnaghane
O'Brosneghan
Brosnahan

BROTHERS
See Broderick

BRUEN   59-68   (15)
See Mac Brine

MAC BRYAN   59   (7)
See Mac Brine

O'BREEN
See Mac Brine

BRYANT   29

BURNS   93-95
O'Beirne
O'Broin   (3-5-6-26-27)
O'Byrne

BUCKLEY   115
O'Buachalla   Norman
O' Buhilly   (18-23-26-27-29)
Bulkley

BURKE	112	BUTCHER	115
de Burca	(13-14-15-19-21-	Bouchier	
De Burgo	23-30)	Boxer	Huguenot
Burc			
<u>Sub Clans</u>:	Norman	BUTLER	113
Mac Coog		le Botiller	Norman
Cook			
Mac Gibbon		O'BYRNE	93 (25)
Mac Hugo		O'Broin	
Jennings			

C

MAC CABE	102 (8-11-18)	MAC CAHEY	115 (4)
Mac Caba	Danish	Mac Eochaidh	
		Mac Caughey	
CADDELL	115	Aghy	
See Blake		Oghay	
		See Hackett	
MAC CADDEN	48		
See Mac Adam		CAHILL	43-71-75
		O'Cathail	(19-22-23-26)
MAC CAFFELLY	40 (6)		
See Mac Guinness		MAC CAHILL	13 (1)
Mac Eachmhilidh		of Donegal	
		A Branch of the	
MAC CAFFERTY	68 (1)	Scotch Campbells	
Mac Eachmharcaigh			
Caffrey		O'CAIRN	97 (3-6)
A Branch of the		O'Ceirin	
Maguires		O'Ciarain	
CAFIE	41	*MAC CALL	13 (4-5)
		Mac Cathmhaoil	
CAFFREY of Cavin	69 (11)	Caffrey	
		Mac Cahill	
MAC CAFFREY	68 (1-4-7)	Caffrey	
Mac Cafraigh			
Mac Gafraidh		CALLANAN	53 (8-9)
Mac Goffrey		Ui Callanain	
		O'Callannan	
O'CAFFY	73 (26)		
O' Cathbhuadhaigh		O'CALLAGHAN	18 (22-27)
Caffee		of Cork	
Caffey		O'Ceallachain	
Coffey		O'Callahan	
O'CAHAN	81 (22)	MAC CALLION	13 (1-8-9)
O' Cathlain		of Donegal	
O'Cein		Mac Callan	
O'Kane		Mac Cailin	
Keane		See Allen	

MAC CALPIN   13   (14)
  of Mayo
See Mac Alpin

CAMBRENSIS, Gerald   108
An Historian   Norman-Welsh

CAMP   13-77   (11)
See Campbell

CAMPBELL   13   (3-4-6)
Mac Cathmaoil
Camp

MAC CANN   25
Mac Ana   (2-3-4-18)

CANNING   29   (2)
O'Coning

CANNON   53-73-88
Ui Canannain   (1-10-14)
O'Cananain of Ulster
O'Canain of Connacht
O'Canann

CANOGY   18

CANTWELL   115
de Cantwell   (18-23-29)
                     Norman

CAOLFIELD   82   (4-7)
Mac Catmaoil
Mac Ceile
Howell

O'CARBHAILL   53   (11)
  of Cavin

O'CARROLL   30-34-65
Ua Cerbhaill   (18-23-27-29-30)
O'Cearbhaill

MAC CARTER   21   (2-3)
See Mac Arthur

CARTHY   20   (25-27)
  of Clann Errought

MAC CARTHY   20   (26)
  of Castle Maine

MAC CARTHY   20
  of Munster   (26-27-30)
Ua Carthaigh
O'Carthy

MAC CARTHY Riabhach 20

MAC CARTHY Mor   19   (19-22)
  of Desmond

CAREY   109
O'Cearig   (14-18-21-23-27)
O'Carra of Galway
Mac Ciolla Ceiret
  of Donegal
Mac Fhirchra
Carr of Donegal
de Carew of Tipparery
O' Ciardha of Kildare
O'Keary

O'CARNEY   24-88   (14)
O'Cearnaigh

O'CARLIN   43   (11-14)
O'Cearbhallain
O'Carleton
Carlan
Carland

MAC CARTAN   39   (2-6)
Mac Cartain
Mac Carten
See Mac Artain

*O' CAROLAN   77   (2-4)
O'Caireallain

CARR   109
Mac Giolla   (1-18-19)
  Chathair
Mac Gillacahir
Mac Elhair
Mac Glare
Mac Ilhair
Kilcarr
See Carey

MAC CARRON   75-82
Mac Carghamhna   (17-29)
Mac Cargamna
Mac Cearain
Mac Caron
See Caufield; Gaffney

CARSON O'Corrghamhna	75	(3-4-6)	O'CEMOG	73	
O'CASEY O'Cathasaigh O'Cahassy O'Casie Catasac	25-41-65 (7-14-15-18- 26-27-30)		CHAMBERLIN Norman-English	115	(27)
			MAC AN CHANUADH	41	
			O'CHERIGH Cherry	74	(6)
O'CASIE See O'Casey	30		CHERRY See Above		
CASH Mac Gillachaise O'Cashin	98	(19-32)	O'CHARNEY See O'Kearney	76	(18-27)
CASS See Cash			MAC CINETH Mac Kenna	93	(3-12)
O'CASSIDY O'Caiside	24-30	(1-3-7)	de CLARE de Cleir Norman	114	(29-32)
O'CAHARNEY See O'Kearney Also Fox of Tiffa	76	(12)	O'CLAIREN O'Cleirchin	22	(30)
CAULFIELD Mac Conghamhna O'Gamhna Mac Conway	13-70 (3-4-8-13)		O'CLANCY Mac Fhannochaidh Mac Flancha Flanagan Flannagain Flinn	14-98 (9-10- 26-27)	
CAVAVAGH O'Caomhain Kavanagh	94 (11-13-14)		Flynn Glenn Glynn Linn		
MAC CAW See Mac Adam	48	(3-11)	Lynn Macklin Maglin Mac Gloin		
MAC CAWELL Mac Eachmhilidh Mac Cathmhaoil See Campbell	76	(4)	CLARK Mac Giolla Arraith Mac Cleirig Mac Clery O' Clery	30-72 (2-3-13)	
MAC CAWLEY Mac Amalgada Mac Amalgaid Mac Auley Caffelly All said to be branches of Mac Guiness Family	40	(17)	CLAUSSON Mac Nioclair Norman	112	
O'CEARIG	73		O'CLEREIN	21	(8)

O'CLERY	30-72	
Mac Clery	(1-18-19)	
Mac anCleirig		
O'Cleiraig		
O'Clerig		
Mac Alary		
Clark of Ulster		
Clarke		
Clerkin		

CLIFFORD	93	(14-26)
O'Clumhain		
of Sligo		
O'Cluvanes		
of Kerry		
Coleman		
Colven		

MAC CLOSKY	81	(1-2)
of Derry		
Mac Bloskey		

O'COALLTAIGH 98

COEN	75	(13)
See Cowen		

COCHRANE	30	(4-6-20)
O'Corcain		
O'Corcrain	Also Scotch	
Mac Corcrain		

O'COFFEY	14	
O'Cathbhuadhaigh	(15-17-18-19-	
O'Cathmhogha	20-23-27)	
O'Cobthaigh		
Coffie		
Cowhey		
Cowie		
Cowhig		

de COGAN 108-110

MAC COUGHLIN	98	(20)
Mac Coghlan		

O'COIRC	48	(27)
of Muskerry		

COLEMAN	93	
O'Clumhain	(15-18-27-28)	
O'Columain		
See Clifford		

O'COLGAN	92	(3-18-20)
of Offaly		
Mac Colgan		

*O'COLLERAN	53	
O'Allmarain		

COLLINS	21	
O'Cuillayne	(4-13-19-	
O'Cuilein	23-27-30)	
Mac Coilin		
Mac Cullen		
Cullinane		
Quillan		

COLLINS	17	
of Sligo	(3-13-19-30)	
O'Cullilleain		
Mac Coileain	Also Norman	
Cullane		

O'COLLOPY	29	(30)
O'Colpa		

MAC COLLVIN	88	
Possibly Houriskey		

COLTER	43-69	(6)
O'Coultarain		
O'Coltrain		
Coltar		

COLVIN	83	(3-4)
Mac Collvin		

COMAIN	73-92	
O'Chomain	(14-27-32)	
Comane		
Cowman		
Hurley		

COMMON	73	(14-19)
See Comain		

O'CONAK 17

O'CONCANNON	29-57	
O'Conceanainn	(14-15-19)	
Branch of O'Briens		
of Galway		

CONAVE	48	(2-3)
See Adams		

CONCHLAIN	98	(27)
O'Coughlain		
O'Cochlain		
CONDON	115	
de Caunteton	(23-26-27-28)	
O'Condubain	Norman	
O'Connduin		
CONLAN	75 (13-14-15)	
O'Caoindealbhain		
Connellan		
See O'Quinlan		
CONLON	82	(15)
O'Conallain		
Conlan		
Conland		
Connellan		
O'CONNELL	17-21-47-69	
Mac Connell	(2-4-19-23-26-27)	
O'Conaill		
O'Conghail		
CONNIRY	53	
O'Conaire		
O'CONNOLLY	25-49	
O'Coingheallaigh	(3-7-8-	
O'Conghalaigh	19-27)	
O'Conghail		
Conley		
Mac Coingeagha		
of Fermanagh		
O'Connell		
Gunning		
O'Connally		
O'CONOR	59-62-76	
of Connacht	(1-14-15-	
Ui Conchobhair	22-26)	
Ui Conchouir		
O'Cancauir		
O'Choncoure		
O'Conghubhy		
O'Konchuir		
O'Konhor		
O'CONOR Don	61	(7)
Branch of O'Conor		
of Connacht		
O'CONOR	30	(2)
of Derry		

*O'CONOR FALY	92	(20)
O'Conor Failghe		
Dec. from Cathaor Mor		
One branch went to Wales		
O'CONOR	21	
of Glenn Geimhin		
O'CONOR	42	(26)
of Kerry		
O'Conchobair		
O'CONOR	41	(22)
of Kilfenora		
O'CONOR ROE	61	(7)
Branch of O'Conor		
of Connacht		
O'CONRICK	75	(19)
O'Conrich		
Mac Annraic		
CONROY?		(8-19)
Conry		
Mac Conri		
CONROY	75	(15-22)
O'Maolconaire		
Mulconry		
CONSIDINE	27	(22-30)
Mac Consaidin		
Branch of the		
O'Briens		
(Mac) CONWAY	41-70	
Mac Conmhaigh	(4-14-22)	
Mac Congamhna		
Caulfield		
MAC COOG		
See Burke		
COOGAN	75	(19)
Ua Cuagain		
O'Comhghain		
Cogan		
Cowan		
Branch of the		
O'Maddens		
COOK	112	(19)
Mac Coog	Norman	
Mac Hugh		
Branch of Hugo Burkes		

O'COONEY	93	
O'Cuanda	(13-14-15)	
COOLEY	65	
O'Cualgne	(3-19-29)	
O'Cuile		
Cowley		
COPLING	93	
Mac Corish	Norman	
See Bermingham		
de COURTENAY	115	
	Norman	
de COURCY	115	
Some changed to:	Norman	
Mac Patrick		
(Mac) O'CORCRAN	32	
	(7-14-26-27)	
COREY	115	(27)
Crew	Norman	
CORLESS	43	(19)
Mag Coirleasa		
Mac Cathail		
Charles		
(O' Mac) CORMAC	24	(23-29)
CORMICAN	24-30	
O'Cormacain	(6-15-19-22)	
Mac Cormack		
in Fermanagh		
MAC CORMAC	24-69	
Mac Cormaic	(7-14-15-23-29)	
	Also Scotch	
CORRIGAN	68	(14-15)
O'Coirecain		
O'Coiricain		
CORRY		(3-22)
O'Comhraidhe		
O'Correy		
See Curry		
MAC CORRY	68	(7)
Mac Gothraigh		

COSGRAVE	69	(8-25)
O'Chosgraidh		
Mac Oscar		
Costello		
*COSTELLO		
See Cosgrave		
MAC COTTER	Danish	(27)
O'Cotter		
COWEN	75	(13)
O'Combain		
O'Cadhain		
O'Comgain		
Coen		
O'Cuain		
Barnacle		
COWLEY	65	(29)
See Cooley		
COWMAN	73	(32)
Mac Comain		
See Cummins		
MAC COY	81	
Mac Cooney	(3-5-8)	
Mac Aooh		
COYNE	75	(13)
O'Cuain		
MAC CRAITH	18	
Mag Raith		
Magrath		
(Mac) CREADY	24	(1)
Mac Riada		
See O'Ready		
O'CREAGH	24-82	(22-30)
O'Craobhach		
O'Craoibhe		
Mac Creagh		
O'Craobac		
O'Creavagh		
of Limerick		
Creigh		
MAC CREDAN	95	(25)
CREADHMACAIN	97	(1)

CREADY 24
McCreery

de CREW   Norman 108

CREGHAN   73   (4-13)
O'Creachain
O'Creacain
O'Cridigan
Creaghan
Crehan

O'CREMIN   21   (26-27)
O'Cruimin
Branch of Mac Carthy

O'CRENNAN   14   (24-29)
O'Crionain

CROFTON   115   (13)
de Croctun   Norman

MAC CROHAN   18   (26)
Mac Criomthainn
Branch of O'Sullivan

CRONIN   18-22
O'Cronain   (26-27-30)
O'Croinin
Cronan

CROWLEY   58   (15-27)
O'Cruadhlaoich

CROCAN   73

CROSBIE   115   (1-2-4)
Mac anCrosain
Mac Acrossane   Norman
Mac Ecrossan
Mac Crossin
Cross

O'CRUCHTA   93

O'CUANDA   93

MAC CUILEAN   98   (22-27)
O'Cuileannain
O'Cuillinan
Mac Cullen

O'CUILLANE   21
(22-27-28)

CUFFIE   63   (27-28)
Duirnin by   English
Mistranslation

O'CUIN   75-98 (13-22)
O'Cuinn
Cowen

*CUITIN   97

CULLANE   17   (30)
O'Coileain
See Collins of Sligo

MAC CULLEN
See Mac Cuilean

MAC CULLEN   98   (8-9)
Mac Cuilean
Mac Cowlin
Mac Collin
Collins
Quillan

O'CULLEN   92   (21)
O'Cuillin

CULLIGAN   30   (22-92)
O'Cuilegain
Mac Colgain
Quilligan

CULLINANE   17   (22-23)
O'Cuileannain
O'Cuillane
O'Quillinane

CULLY   65   (3-5)

MAC CULREAVY   56   (16)
Mac Cathail Riabhaigh

CUMMINS   74   (27-32)
 of Cork
O'Comain
O'Comin
Mac Comin
Commons of Wexford
Comyn
O'Cuimin of Connacht
Cowman
Hurley

O'CUNING   93   (20)
O'Coinin
Kenyon

CUNNINGHAM   75-76
O'Congadhain   (3-6-15-18-19-27)
O'Connagain
O'Connegan
Mac Conegan
At least two Irish branches
plus an English family

CURNEEN   29   (10)
O'Cuirnin

O'CURNIN   13   (10-26)
O'Curneen of Kerry

O'CURRAN   69   (23-28)
O'Currane
O'Curreen
O'Currain
Mac Carrain

O'CURRY   43   (22-27)
O'Corraidhe

(Mac) O'CURRY   24   (3)
O' Comhraidhe
Also Scotch name Currie

MAC CUTCHEON   65   (3-4-6)
Mac Uistin
Also Scotch

ð

DALE of Ulster   17
See O'Dell

O'DALLAGHAN   88
 of Connacht
O'Dalachan

O'DALY   18-68-77-87
O'Dalaigh   (17-27)
Daily
Daley
Dawley
Dawlie

O'DANBIG   69

MAC DANIEL   20   (26)
 of Barrett
 Branch of the
 Mac Carthys

DARBY   76   (1-2)
O'Dubhderma
O' Duibhdhiorma
See O'Dermod

DARCY   41   (7-14)
Mac Dorchaidh
O'Dorcy

O'DAUGHERTY   87   (1)
O'Dochartaigh
Dade
Darty
Dougherty
Doherty

MAC DAVID   58   (15)
Branch of Mac Dermot

DAVIDSON
See Mac Davitt

O'DAVIN   69
O'Daimhin   (7-22-23)
Devin

DAVIS   94
Mac Daibhis   Welsh
O'Morchoe

MAC DAVITT   17-58-87-94-112
Mac Daibheid   (1-2-14-32)
Mac Daibhith
Mac Daibeid   Norman
Mac David
Davidson
Davies
Davis
Davy, a branch of deBurgo
Dawson
Day

O'DAVOREN 22 (22)
O'Dubhdabhoirenn 17
O'Babhoireann

DAWSON
See Mac Davitt

DAY 98 (22-26)
O'Deabelow
O'Deaghaidh
O'Diaghaidh
O'Dea
O'Dead
O'Deady of Kerry
O'Day of Clare
See Mac Davitt

O'DEADHAICHD 98 (26)
Possibly O'Deaghaidh
 and O'Dea
See Day

*DEANE 88
O'Deagain (1-19-23)
de Denne Norman
Mag an Deaganaig
 a branch of O'Donnell

O'DEE 98 (23-28)

MAC DEENEY 81 (1)
Mac Avinue

O'DEENEY 71 (1-2)
Mac aPhobuill
O'Duibhne

O'DEENY 71 (19)
O'Duibgiolla Norman
de Villy

DELAHUNTY 30 (20)
See O'Dulanty

O'DELANY 97 (29)
O'Dubhshlaine

O'DELL 17 (30)
English

DEMPSEY 92 (20-24)
O'Dimusaig
O'Diomasaig
Branch of O'Conor Failge

DENNY 115 (26)
de Villy Norman

O'DEREMASACH 93

O'DERMOND 76 (1-2)
O'Duibhdhioraome
O'Duibhdhiora
Darby

MAC DERMOTT 58
O'Duibdiorma (2-4-15-19)
O'Duibdiormaig
O'Dughierma
O'Darby
Dermond
Mac Dermot Roe
O'Dermott
Mac Diarmada
O'Diorma
O'Duvdirma

DEVAN 30 (13)
See Downs

O'DEVANNY 97 (1)
Dhuineamhla

O'DEVINE 41 (4-15)
O'Dubhain
O'Daimhin
O'Devane
O'Devaney

O'DEVLIN 77
O'Doibhilin (3-4-13)
de Moleyns Norman

DICOLO 93

O'DIFF 29 (14)
O'Dubhthaigh
 of Munster
O'Doithe
O'Doohig
O'Duffy

DILLON 76-77
O'Dubhsblaine (15-17-30)
O'Duilleain Norman?
Dillane

O'DINDON 92 (30)
de Auno Norman
Dondon

DINEEN   91   (26)
See Downing

O'DOIRE   76   (30)
O'Dogair
Dore

DOLAN   97   (19)
O'Dholbhain

MAC DONAGH   21-25-92
Mac Donnchadha   (19-27)
Branch of Mac Carthy

MAC DONALD   68   (7)
Mac Domhnull

DONEGAN   65   (1)
See Duncan

O'DONIVAN   17   (27-30)
O'Donnabhain
O'Donovan

DONLEVY   (1)
O'Duinnsleibhe
Mac Duinntshleibhe
hEocada
Hoey
Hoy
A non-Gaelic name

MAC DONNELL   65
Mac Domhnaill   (3-19-22)
                      Scotland

O'DONNELL   88   (1)
O'Domhnaill

DONNELLY   76-80
O'Donnghaile
O'Dunghaile
Donley

MAC DONOGH   58   (14-15)
  of Connacht
Mac Donnchadh
Branch of Mac Dermott

DONOGHUE   18-22
O'Donnchadha   (11-26-27)
Donahoe
Dunphy

O'DONOGHUE   93   (18)
  of Dublin

O'DOOLAN   32-94   (19)
O'Dubhlainn
O'Dolhonty
O'Donnalan
Dowling

DOOLEY   31   (17-20)
Ui Dubhlaigh
O'Dubhlaoich
O'Dubhalla
O'Doorly

DOONAN   40
O'Dunain   (7-10-15)

O'DORAN   18   (6-32)
O'Dheorain

O'DOREY   43   (30)

O'DOREY of Ulster   65

DORNAN   62   (3-6-9)
O'Dornain
See Durning

DOWD   74
O'Dubda   (2-13-26)
  of Derry
O'Doody   English
  of Kerry
Doud
Duddy
O'Neill

O'DOWDA   73   (14)
O'Dowd
O'Dubhda

O'DOWEL   73   (15)
Mac Dubhghaill
Doyle

DOWLING
See O'Doolan   English

DOWNING   91   (2-26)
O'Dunadhaigh
O'Duinin
O'Duinnin
Dineen
MacDowney

DOWNS	30-43	
O'Duain	(13-14-30)	
O'Duana		
Donan		
Doon		
Dwane		
Hooke		

DRENNAN 21 (19-23)
O'Draighnean
Thornton
  in Galway

O'DRISCOLL 14 (27)
O' hEidersceoil

DUAINE 30 (13)
See Downs

O'DUAN 43-82 (19)
O'Dubhain
Duane

O'DUBAN 93
See O'Duggan

DUDDY 74
Doddy
See O'Dowd

MAC DUFFIE 29 (1-3-8)
Mac Duibsite
Mac Duffyhe
Mac Affie
Mac Affee
  of Antrim

DUFFY 29-92
O'Dubhthaigh (1-8-14-26-27)
O'Duibhe
O'Doithe
  of Mayo
Doohey
Duig

MAC DUGALL 65 (15)
Mac Dubgaill Scotch
Doyle

O'DUGAN 92
Ua Dubhagain (1-4-19-27)
O'Dubhagain
O'Duggan
Doogan

O'DUGGAN 93 (1)
O'Dubhagain
O'Duban

O'DUHIG 29 (26-27)
See Duffy

O'DUIGENAN 75
O'Duibhgeannain (11-15-16)

O'DULANTY 115 (20)
O'Dulchaoinitigh
la Ahunty Norman

DULLARD 115 (18)
Dollard

DUMPHY 22 (29)
O'Donnchaidh
O'Donoghue

DUNCAN 65 (1)
Donnagain Scotch
Donegan

MAC DUNLEVY 43 (1-6)
Mac Duinnshleibhe
Dunlap
  in Scotland
See O' hEochy

DUNN 53
O'Doyle (2-4-11-24-27)
O'Duinn

DUNNEEAN 82 (10-23)
O'Donnagain
O'Dongane
O'Dunegan

DUNPHY
See Donoghue

O'DHUIRNIN 62 (1-3-7)
O'Duirnin
Durming
Durnan
O'Durlyne
Dunyen
O'Dornin
O'Dornan
Durning

O'DURACK 29 (22)

138

DWAIN   30   (13)   O'DWYER   91   (23)
See Downs   Duibhir

e

O'EAKIN   65   (2-6)   MAC ENNRY   53   (19)
Aiken   Mac Einri   Norman
                                        See Mac Henry
EDDERLY   115 (14)
Mac an Ridire   ENRIGHT   24-69 (22)
Eddery   Norman   Mac Ionnractaig
Branch of Fitzsimmons   O'Henrighta
                                        O'Henrighty
MAC EDMOND   110
Mac Eammoinn   MAC EOCAID   19
Mac Aimon   Anglo-Irish   Mac Oghie
                                        Mac Eochy
MAC EGAN   48-69-73
Mac Aodhagain   (18-19-20-23)   MAC EOCHADH   43
Mac Adacain   of Linster
O'Caogain   Mac Keogh
Mac Eagan
Mac Eagin   O'EOGAIN   59-93 (15)
Keegan   Mac Owen
Mac Egan   Hogan?

MAC ELHAIR   109 (1)   MAC EVILLY   115
Mac Giolla Chathair   See Stonton
See Carr   Mac Avey   Norman
                                        Mac Elwee
MAC ELLIOGOTT   21   (26)   Mac Evoy
Mac Uileagoid   Norman   Ilwee
                                        Gilloway
ENNIS   92   (17)   Gilboy
O' hAongusa   Magillow
O' Haonghus   Mac Giolla Bruide
Enos
Hennessy

f

MAC FABRENE   110   O'FAHY   73   (19)
                Norman
                                        O'FAILBE   48 (22-27)
O'FABY   74   of Cork
                                        O'Falvey
O'FAHERTY   41   (19)   of Kerry
O'Fathartaigh
                                        O'FAIRY   76 (1-13)
                                        O'Fearadhaigh

O'FALLON	57-93		O'FENAN	97
UiFallamhain	(5-6-15-19)		of Connacht	
O'Fallamain				

MAC FEORAIS 115
Forrest
See de Bermingham

O'FALVEY   47 (26-27)
O'Failbhe

O'FERCINN   98 (22)
Perkins

FANNON   18-20
O'Fionnain   (15-19-23-30)
Mac Finighan
Mac Flonneen
O'Finan
O'Fainin

FERRAND   115 (3-6)
Mac Mhearain   Norman

O'FAOLAIN   50 (15)
O'Fallamhain
Whelan

FERRIS   17 (26)
of Kerry   Scotch
O'Fergus

FARNHAM   (4)
O'Fhorannan
O'Forann
O'Farnon

MAC FHILIB   66 (3)
Branch of Mac Sorley

O'FINAN   20
O' Fionnain

O'FARRELL   86 (16)
O'Fearghail
O'Farrill

MAC FINGIN   20 (26)

O'FARRELLY   68 (11-12)
O'Faircheallaigh

O'FINGIN   18 (23)
of Cashel

O'FARRILL   41 (25)
O'Feargail
O'Fearall

O'FINN   92
O' Fionn   (8-13-19)

FAY
See O'Fahy

O'FINNAGHTY   57 (15)
Fionnachta
O'Finnerty
Finaghty

O'FEALL   92
O'Feadhail

O'FINNOC   53 (15)

O'FEARDIG   93

MAC FIRBISE   70 (13-14)
Mac Firbhisigh
Mac Firbiegh
Mac Firbise
of Lecan
Forbes

O'FEE   77 (7-11)
O'Fiaich
O'Fiachnach
O'Foy
Hunt

FITZBERNARD   115
Norman

FEENEY   82 (13-15)
O'Fighe

FITZGERALD   109
Mac Gerailt   (21-32-27-28-30)

MAC FELAN   69 (28-29)
O'Faolain
O'Phelain

FITZGIBBON   112
Also a branch of   Norman
Burke

FITZGILBERT 114
Norman

FITZGODBERT 115
Norman

FITZGRIFFIN 109
Norman

FITZMORRIS 109 (14-26)
Mac Muiris
See Pendergasts
of Mayo

FITZOTHER 108
Otho Norman

FITZPATRICK 43-97 (7)
of Ossory
Mac Giolla Phadraig
Mac Gillarvig

FITZSIMMONS 115 (6-14)
Assumed the name Norman
Edderly

FITZWILLIAM 112
Mac William Norman

O'FLAHERTY 69-77 (1-4)
of Ailech
O'Flaithbheartaigh

O'FLAHERTY 25-76 (26)
of Kerry
O'Flaithbheartaigh

O'FLANAGAIN 83
of Toorigh

FLANAGAN 98 (22)
Flannagain
Flinn
Flynn
See O'Clancy

O'FLANAHY 13-14 (22)
Mac Flannchaidh

FLANERY 21 (14-30)
O'Flannabhra

O'FLANNAGAIN 30
of Cinel Arra (7-15-17)

O'FLANNAGAIN 57-85 (15-22)
of Roscommon

O'FLANNAGAIN 69 (17-23)
of Westmeath

O'FLATHERTY 41-64 (19-22)
of Connacht
O'Flaithbheartaigh

le FLEMING 115
Norman

FLINN
FLYNN
See O' Clancy

O'FLOINUS 92 (20)

MAC FLONNEEN 20
See O' Finan

FLOOD 91 (22)
Mac Maoltuile
Mac Atilla
Mac Tully

FLYNN 65 (4)
of Ulster

O' FLYNN 13-98
of Ards (3-15-27-32)
O'Floinn
of Wexford
O' Fhloinn
of Antrim
O'Lynn

O'FOGARTY 21-82-85 (23)
O'Maol Fogarty
O'Fogartaigh
Fogerty

FOLAN 54 (19)
O'Floinnlinne
Mac Floaine
Mac Fualain

O'FOLLACHTY 92

FORAN 92 (27)
O'Foranan
O'Fuarain

g

FORBES	70	(22)
Forbis	Scotch	
See Mac Firbise		

FORD 48-55 (18-19)
Mac Consnamha
Mac Consnave
Mac Consnava
Mac Giolla na Naomh
Mac Giollarrath
Mac Aneave
Mac Anata
Mac Kinnawe
  of Lough Allen
See Mac Adam; Mac Elnay

FORENAN 97 (26)
O'Fhorannan
O'Forannain

FOX 25-84
O'Siodhachain (4-9-17-20-29)
O'Catharnaig
O'Sionna of Westmeath
Mac Ashinah
Mac Shanaghy of Louth
O'Shonogh
Shinnock of Kilkenny
Kearney

FOY 77
O'Fiaich (11-14-18)
See O' Fee

FRAZER (27)
See Barron Norman

FRENCH 115
O' Fraechain (15-19-32)
Franche Norman
de Freyne

O'FRIEL 86 (1)
O'Firghil
O'Freel

O'FUREY 84 (17-19)
O'Fiodhabhra
O'Foirreith

O'GADHRA 30-34 (13-14)
O'Gara of Sligo
O'Gadra of Luighne
Branch of O'Hara

GAFFNEY 13 (8)
O'Gamhna
Mac Conghamhna
Caulfield
Mag Fhachta
Gaughney
See Mac Carron

GAHAN 68 (25-32)
O'Gaoithin
Mac Gaoth
Gaughan

MAC an GAIVNIOV 43 (11)
See Smith

GALLAGHER 89 (1)
O'Gallchobhair
O'Galligher

MAC GAOTH 68
See Gahan

MAC GARRAN 39-95 (1-5-7)
Magarghain
Mag Eacrain
Ui Garrchon
  of Linster
Magarghain

GARRITY 57 (15)
Mag Oireactaig
Mageraghty

O'GARVEY 67-69-76
O'Gairbhith (4-6-14-26)
O'Garbhain
O'Garvin
Also branches of
  O'Hanlun and Moriarty

O'GARVIN 17 (26)
O'Garbhain

O'GARY 32 (10-15)
Mag Fheardhaigh
Garry
Mac Hughes of
  Connacht

O'GAUGHNEY 13
See Gaffney

GAYNOR   93   (16)
Mac Fhionnbhairr
Mac Ginty
Mac Ginver

O'GERAN   93   (30)
Guerin
See Green

GERARD   109
                        Norman

de GERNEMIE   115
                        Norman

O'GERY   30   (27)
O'Gadhra

MAC GIBBON   112
Mac Giobuin   Norman
Gibbons
Branch of Burke

O'GILBEY   59   (18)
O' Giolla Buidhe
Gilboy   Norman-Scotch
Ogilvy

GILBOY   115
See Stonton   Norman

MAC GILFIN   32   (13)
Mac Giolla Finn
Mac Gilpin

GILKINSON
Mac Uilicin   Norman-Scotch
See Mac Quilkin

MAC GILL   112   (29)
Mac an Ghill
Gaules
Branch of Burke

MAC GILLICK   112   (11)
Mac Uilic
Branch of Burke

MAC GILLICUDDY   18   (26)
Mac Giolla Chuda
Gilla Mochuda

GILLIGAN   43-98
Mac Giolla Gain   (2-11-13)
O'Gealagain
 of Sligo
Gillan
White of Cavin

O' GILLORAN   25 (13-15)
Mac Giolla Luaighrin
Killoran of Sligo

GILMARTIN   80   (4-7)
Mac Giolla Mhartain
Branch of O'Neills
 of Tyrone

MAC GILMER   41   (6)
Mac Giollamhuire
Gilmore
Branch of O'Morna

MAC GINNESS   40   (6)
Magennis
See Mac Guinness
 of Down

MAC GINTY   93   (8-16)
Mac Fhionnbhairr
See Gaynor

MAC GINVER   93   (16)
See Gaynor

MAC GILLA LAISIR   51

MAC GILPIN
See Mac Gilfin

MAC GIVNEY   81   (11)
See Mac Avinue

GLANCHY   69
Mag Flanncada
Maglanchy
See Mac Gorry
Branch of Mac Namara

de GLANVIL   115
                        Norman

GLENN   98   (22)
Glynn
See Clancy

MAC GLOIN	98	(1)
Mac Giolla Eoin		
Monday		

O'GLORNEY	25	(29)
O'Glothairne		
O'Gloiairn		

GODFREY	69	(7)
Mac Gorry		
Mac Gotraid		
Mac Curry		
Branch of Maguire		

MAC GOFFREY	68	(7)
See Mac Caffrey		

GOLDEN	57	(10)
Mag Ualghairg		
Mac Goldrick		
Branch of O'Ruarc		

MAC GOLDRICK	78
Mag Ualghairg	

GORDON	54	(6)
Mag Mhuirneachain		
Magournahan		
Maguran		

O'GORMAN	82	(1)
See Gormley		

O'GORMAN	91-92
Mac Gorman	(8-22-24)
of Leix	

O'GORMLEY	82
Ua Gairmleadhaigh	
O'Gormshuiligh	(1-14-15)
O'Gormshuil	
O'Gormooly	
Gormilly	
Gorman of Donegal	

MAC GORRY	69	(11)
Mac Gothraidh		
Corry		

MAC GOVERN	54	(11)
Mag Samirain		

MAC GOWAN	38
Mac an Ghabhann	(1-10-11-23)
Mac Gabhann	
Smith	
Smithson	

GRACE	109	(29-32)
le Gras	Norman	

O'GRADY	98
O'Gradaigh	(14-22-30)
Brady	

MAC GRANUILL	43	(32)
Mac Grannel		
Mac Ragnall		
Mac Reynolds		
See Mac Rannell		

O'GRAVEY	76

GREEN	24
O' hUainin	
Huainain	
Honeen	

GRIFFIN	93-98 (22-21)
O'Griobhtha	
Griffyn	
Griffey	

GRIFFITH	107-109
See Griffin	Welsh

GRIMES	76-82	(4-7)
O'Goirmleadaigh		
of Ulster		
O'Gormghaile		
of Connacht		
Gormally		
Gormley		

le GROS	109
	Norman

O' GUBAN	92
See Smith	

GUCKIN	115
See Hackett	Norman

MAC GUIRK Mac Oric	82	(4)	GUTHBINN See O'Bannon	83	(7)
O' GUNNING O' Conaing See O' Connolly	25	(27)	GUTHRIE Guthrigh Lahill	68	(22)

h

O'HACHLERNE See Ahern	25	(27)	HAMILL O' Hadhmaill O' hAomaill	76	(3-4-8)
HACKETT Hacum Haiceid Mac Cahey Mac Hackett Guckin	115	(21-29) Anglo-Norman	HANAHAN See Bird O'HANBY	115 43-69	(18)
O'HADIN See O' hEidin	72	(15)	HANEY Mac Aney See Bird	115	
O'HAGAN O' hAodhagain O' Faodhagain Aiken Eagain of Linster Hog Huggin Uggin	76-77 (3-4-18)		O'HANIGAN O' hAnnagain O'HANLEY O' hAinlidhe O' hAinle O' Handly See Ainly	95 53-98	(25-28) (15-22-27)
HAGERTY O' hEigeartaigh O'Hegarty	18	(27)	O' HANLON O' hAnluain See Garvey	67	(5)
O'HAGLERN Ahern	25	(22)	HANRAHAN O' hAnracain O' Hanragain Hanracan	25-93	(22)
HALEY O' hAlgaith	25	(27)	O'HARA O' Headhra O' hEagra O' Gara	30	(13)
HALLINAN O' hAilgheanain O' Hallin O' Hallion See Mac Allen	13 (23-28-30) 17		O'HARE O' Hehir O' Aichir Hegar	17	(22-30)
O' HALLORAN O' hAllmhurain O' hAlluchain	29	(19-22)			
HALLY O' hAilche	25	(23)			

O' HARGAIN O' hArgain Hourigan Harrigan	41	(27-30)
O' HAROLD O' hArailt	102 Norse	(18-30)
O' HART O' hAirt	52-92	(13)
HARTIGAN O' hArtagain O' Hartaig	92	(22-30)
HASTINGS de Hastings O' Huisgin O' Hiskeen	115 Norman	
O' HAY de la Haye de Hay O' hAodha Hayes	82-115 (27-32) Norman	
HAYDEN Ui Aodain O' hEidain	72-93 (15-31-32) Norman	
O' HAYS O' hEddhasas See O' Hay	38 (1-4-14)	
O' HEA O' hAodha Fearlurg	88	(27)
O'HEADY	98	
O' HEAFFIE Mahaffie	98 Scotch	(30)
O' HEAGHER O' hAichir O' Hehir	17	(22-30)
O' HEALY O' hEilighe	41	(22)
O' HEANEY O' hEignigh O' Heagny O' Hegny	65	(7)

O' HEASY	82	
HEFFERNAN O' hIfearnain	98 (22-23-30)	
O' HEGARTY of Ulster O' hEigceartaigh O' Hegerty	18-22	
O' HEGLERN O' Hachierne See Ahern	25	(22)
O' HEIR Hare	21	(22)
HENDRICK Mac Annraic	94	(32)
HENNESSY Ua hAenghusa O' hAonghusa Mallow See Ennis	92 (18-20-27)	
O'HENRIGHTY See Enright	69	
HENRY See Bird	115	
MAC HENRY Mac Einri	81	(19)
O' HEOCHY Mac Dunnshleibhe Mac Dunlevy	43	(1)
O'HERN O' hEarain O'Heran	25	(5)
O' HESSON See Osian	97	(14-19)
HESTAND O' hOistin Hastings	58	(14)
O'HEYNE O' hEidhin	72	(19)
HICKEY O' hIcidhe	29	(22)

O' HIGGINS 24
O' hUigin (13-19-22)

HINDS 24-71 (19)
O'Heyne Welsh
Mac Keown
Owens

HINNIGAN 29 (14)
O' hEineachain
O' Hennighan
Henaghan

HOG
See O' Hagan

HOGAN 25-67 (23-27)
O' hEochagan
O' hOgain

HONEEN
See Green

HOOKE 30 (13)
See Downs

O' HOOLAHAN 41-92
O' Huallachain (7-20-22-27)
O'Houlihan
Mac Cuolahan
Holohan
Nolan

HORTON 82 (14)
O' hOdhrain
O' hOirtin
O' Fhorannain
Horan

HOURICAN 25 (16)
O' hAnnrachain

HOUSTON 65 (1)
Mac Quiston English
Mac Taghlin

HOWARD 17-102 (13)
O' hIomhair Danish
O' hIomhain
O' hLomair
Ivers Norman-English
Ivors
Hever

HOWE 56 (7)
O' hEogain
Hayes
Hone English
O' Howen
See O' Hoey

HOWELL
See Caolfield

HOWLEY 14 (27)
Whooley

HOWTH 115 (22)
de St. Laurence Norman

HOY
Hoey
See Donlevy

MAC HUGH 56-64-68-111
Mac Aodha (7-10-19)
Mac Hugo Norman
Hughes
See O' Gary

HUGHES
See Mac Hugh

MAC HUGO
See Burke

HUNT 77
O' Fiaich
See O' Fee

HURLEY 24-73 (22-27)
O' hUrthuile
Commons
Murley
Urtaile
See O'Chomain

U' HUSSY 76 (4-7)
O' hEodhusa
O' Hosey

HUTCHINSON 65 (6)
Mac Cutcheon
Mac Uistin Scotch
Huston
Kitchen
Branch of Mac Donald

HYNES 56-72
O' Heyne (14-19-22)

í

MAC ILLASHER	68	(7)	IORADAIN	97	
Mac Giolla Laisir			See O' Riordan		
A branch of Maguire					
			MAC IVER	102	(9-18)
MAC INIRY	25	(22)	Mac Iomhair	Norse	
Mac an Airchinnigh					
Mac Inerney			IVERS		
Nerney			Ivor		
			See Howard		
IONNMHASAIGH	97				

j

JENNINGS	112	(14-19)	JERETY	57	(17)
Mac Shgoinin			See Garrity		
Mac Seinin					
Mac Keoneen			JOHNSON	80	Ulster
Branch of Burke			of the Fews		
			Mac Shane		
			Branch of O'Donnell		

k

O'KANE	81	(2-4)	KEARNEY	29-43-76-88	
O' Cathain			O' Catharnaigh	(23)	
O' Cahan			O' Cearnaigh		
			O' Kearny		
KARR	109	(19)	Fox of Meath		
O' Carra					
			O' KEEFE	18	(27)
KAVANAGH	94	(32)	O' Caoimit		
O' Caomhanach					
See Cavanagh			KEEGAN		
			See Mac Egan		
O' KEADY	73	(19)			
Mac Keady			MAC KEEVER	69	(8)
Mac Ceadaigh			Mac Eimhir		
KEAN	82	(28)	O' KEITHERNY	41	
O' Cein					
Keane			O' KELAGHAN	18	(8-9)
			Ua Celechain		
O'KEANE			Ua Cellachain		
O' Kane					
See O' Cahan			KELLER	25	(26-27)
			O' Ceileachair		
			O' Kelleher		

O'KELLIE   68
O' Kelly

O'KELLY   19-57-68-76
O' Ceallaigh   (4-19)

KEMP   13-77
See Campbell

O'KENDELLAN   75   (9)
O' Kendillon
Kindellan   Spain
See Quinlan

MAC KENNA   93 (31-32)
O' Enda
O'Ena
Mac Eanna
See Mac Cineth

KENNEDY   25 (22-32)
O' Cinneide   Scotch

KENNELLY   17-41-48
O' Cinnfhaolaidh
Connelly
Kinnealy
Quinnelly

O'KENNY   43 (1-19)
 of Ulster
O'Cionaoith

KENNYON   29
O' Coning
See Canning

KENYON   93
See O'Cuning

MAC KENZIE   108
         Scotch
    Norman-Welsh

MAC KEOGH   19-32-58
See Mac Eochaidh (15-23-25)

MAC KEON   115   (3)
 of Antrim
See Bissett

O'KERIN   73
O' Ciarain
Kieran

MAC KERMODE   58 (15-19)
Branch of Mac Dermott

KERNEY   75
O' Ceitearnaig (1-15-27)
O' Cithernig
Kerns

O'KERWIC   21   (29)
See Kirby

KIELTY   98

MAC KIERNAN   61   (7)
Mac Thighearnain
Mac Tiernan

KILBRIDE   29
Mac Giolla Brighde
Mac Gilbride
See Mac Bride

KILLIAN   93
O' Cillin (6-14-19-22)
Killine

MAC KILLOP   66   (3)
Mac Fhilib

KILLORAN   25 (13-15)
Mac Giolla Loaighrinn
Mac Killoran
See O' Gilloran

KINEAVY   48
Kinnavy

KING   98
Conray

MAC KINNAWE   48
Mac Conshnamha
See Ford

O'KINNEALY   17 (30)
O' Cinnfhaolaidh
O' Kinneally

MAC KINNEY   69 (4-7)
Mac Coinnigh   Scotch
Mac Kenzie
Mac Kinna

MAC KINLEY 41 (3)
Mac an Leagha
Mac Alee
Kinlay

KINNSELLA 94
O' Cinnsealaig (21-22-32)
O' Cinselaigh
O' Kynsillaghe
Kinsley

KINSLEY 91
See Kinsella

KIRBY 21-93 (29-30)
O' Ciarmac
O'Ciarmhail
O'Ciarba
Kerwick
Kerby

KITCHEN
See Hutchinson

MAC KNIGHT 115 (17)
See Mac Ruddery

KNOWLAN 50-69-93
O' Nowlan (16-17)
See O' Nolan

L

O'LACERY 13

LACKEN 93
O' Lalcain
O' Lacain

de LACY 115 (30)
Norman

O' LADIN 53 (10)

O'LAIGHEN 25 (26)
O'Laoghain

LANE 53 (19)
O' Laigin
O' Ladin
Lyons

MAC LANE 98 (3)
Mac Giolla Eain
Mac Clean
Mac Lean

LARKIN 18-25-69
O' Lorcain (8-19-23-32)
O'Lorcan
See Lawson

de ST. LAURENCE 115 (22)

LAVERTY 43 (1-4)
O' Laithbheartaigh
O' Lafferty

O'LAVERTY 73 (1-4)
O' Flaherty

MAC LAVERTY 77 (1-4)
Mac Fhlaithbheartaigh

O' LAWLER 43
O' Leathlobhair
O' Lalor

LAWRENCE 25
English
From Lancashire

LAWSON 18
O' Labhras
Larkin

LEAMY · 23 (23)
O' Laomdha
O' Lemagh
O' Leime

MAC LEAN 92
Mac Ailin

O'LEARY 13-14 (15-27)
O' Laoghaire

LEAVY 41 (16)
Mac con Shleibhe

LEE   25-56
O' Laidhigh
O' Laoidhigh

ST. LEGER   113
        Norman-English
      German in Limerick

O'LENNAN   73 (19-27)
O' Leannain
O' Linneen
Leonard

MAC LEOD   5
 of Scotland

LEONARD   73-89-92 (7-27)
Mac Giolla Fhinnein
Mac Alioion
Mac Aleenen
Allian
O' Lennan
See Mac Dermott

MAC LEWELYN   115
See Mac Quillan Norman-Welsh

O' LICANC   75

O'LIDDY   98   (22)
O' Lideadha

LINCH   24   (1)
 of Donegal
O' Loingseachain
O' Lynchehain
Branch of Scotch
 Mac Clintock

LINDSEY   24 (3-11)
O' Loinsigh
Linchey
Linch
Lynch

O'LINNANE   97
O' Linneain
O' Lionnain

LINNEEN   73
See O'Lennan

LOFTUS   30
O' Lachtnain
Loughnane   English

LOGAN
O' Leoghain
See Lohan

LOHAN   18 (19)
O' Leochain
O' Lochin
Loghan
O' Lohan
O' Loughlin
Logan

(O') MAC LONAIN 72
Lenane

O'LONERGAIN 25 (23-30)
O' Longargain

LONG   69-75
O'Longachain (5-14-27-30)
O' Longaigh
O' Longain
O' Lonagan

LONGSPEAR   106
      Norman

MAC LONS   88

LOONEY   68 (22)
O' Luanaigh
See Bright and
 O' Lunin

O' LORCAN   69
O' Lorchain (8-19-23-32)
O' Larkin
Branch of O'Maddon
 of Galway

O' LOSCAN   93

O'LOUGHLIN   85 (1)
O' Maoil Scachlainn
O' Melaghlin
Mac Laughlin of Clann
 Coleman

O' LOUGHLIN 42-58 (22)
 of Corcumore
Branch of Mac Dermott

MAC LOUGHLIN	41-78
O' Loghlin	(1-2-23)
of Boireann	
O' Lochlann	
of Tipperary	

| LOWNEY | 18 | (27) |
| Leamhnah | | |

O' LUNIN	68
O' Linneen	(7-19-27)
O' Leannain	
Lennon	
Lynegar	
See Bright and Looney	

O'LUNNY	18
O' Luanaigh	
O' Luineach	
O' Luinigh	

O'LYN	43-98	(31)
O' Laigheanain		
Linn		
O' Lynam		
O' Yam		

LYNCH	24-43
de Lench	(3-11-14-27)
O' Longsigh	
O' Loinsy	Norman
Mac Clintock	

LYNHAM	25	(31)
O' Laighen		
O' Lean		
Lyons		

O'LYNN	13	(3)
O' Fhloinn		
See O' Flynn		

LYONS	17-25
O' Laighen	
O' Liathain	
Lehan	
Lynam	
Lyne	

MAC LYSAGHT	28	(22-30)
Mac Giolla Iasachta		
Mac Gilleseaghtie		
Mac Gilly Saghtee		
Mac Lisaght		

m

MACKAY	68	(23)
Mac Aedha		
Mac Hugh		
Mackie?		

MACKLIN	98	(22)
Maglin		
Mac Gloin		
See Clancy		

| MACNIE | 13 | (23) |
| See Neville | | |

| O'MADDON | 75 | (19) |
| O' Madadhain | | |

MADDOX	94	(32)
of Wexford		
Mac Mhadoc		
Maddock		

MAGEE	68-73
Mac Aodha	(3-5-17)
Mac Gee	
Magaoth	

MAGEOGHEHAN	75	(17)
Mac Geoghegan		
Mag Eochagain		

MAGILL	71	Ulster
Mac an Ghaill	English	
Mac Gill		

MAGINNIS	38	(6)
Mag Aonghusa		
Mac Ginness		
Mac Guinness		
Mac Guinnes		
Mag Ennise		

MAGRATH 18-68
Mac Gragh (1-6-7-22-28)
of Donegal
Mac Graw
of Down
Mac Graith
Mac Grath
See Mac Craith

MAGUIRE 68 (7)
Maguidhir

MAGURAN 54 (1-5-8)
Mac Gawran
See Gordon

MAHAFFIE 98 (1)
Mac Dhuibhshithe
See O' Heaffie

MAHER 30 (20-23)
O' Meachair
O' Meghar

MAC MAHON 67-69 (8-22)
Mac Mathghamhna
Mathews

MAC MAHON 58
of Kilelmeaky
O' Matgamna

O' MAHONY 18-22 (14-27)
O' Mathghamhana
O' Mahoney

O' MAHONY 26 (22)
of Clare

O'MAILTOLLA 18
O' Mahoil Tolla

O'MAINE 25-92 (17)
O' Manny
of Westmeath

O'MALLEY 53 (14)
O' Maille
O' Mayle

MALLON 22-80-91
O' Meallain
See O' Mullen

MALLON 92 (3)
O' Melain
O' Mellain

O'MALLONE 59-92
O' Maoileoin (20-22)
O'Mallone
Muldoon of Clare

MALLOW
See Hennessy

MALONE 48
Magiolla Eocain (18-22-32)
Monday
Mac Lune

O'MALONY 24 (23)
O' Maoldhomhnaigh
Maloghney
O' Molony
Mac Loughney

O' MANAHAN 39-56
O' Mainchin (15-22)
Manihan
Mannix
Minogue
Monk

MANDEVILLE 115 (3-23)
de Moinbhiol
See Mac Quillan

MANNING 41-92 (19)
O' Mainnin
O'Mannin
O' Maining

MANNIX 39 (7-22)
O' Manahan

O' MANNY 25

MAC MANUS 59-68 (7-15)
Mac Maghnuis

UI MAOILCOIN 91

O'MAOLMONY 88

O' MAOLSIONNA 75

MARKELL	115 Norman	
MAC MASTER	56	(7)
MATHER O' Maghair O' Meacair	86	(23)
MATHEWS Mac Mathghamhna Mac Mahon of Clare	27-69	(8)
MAC MAURICE See Prendergast	115 Norman	
MAY Meagh Branch of Condon	115 English-Norman	(27)
O' MEAGHER O' Meachair	30-31	(20-23)
O' MEARA O' Meadhra	24	(23)
O'MEEGAN O' Midhagain O' Mihan See O' Meehan	21	(9)
O' MEEHAN O' Miadhachain O' Mecan Meeghan O' Miothan Thornton	17-21	(7)
MEGARACHAIN O' Mhegarachain	39	
O' MELAGHLIN O' Maoilsheachlainn	84	(12)
MELLON O' Mellain O' Melain O' Mellan Mallon	76-77-80-92	(3-4)
MELVILLE O' Mulfoyle Mac Faal Mac Paul Levelle	76 Norman	(1)

MERNAGH of Wexford	94	(25-32)
O' MHEADHA See O' Meara		(27)
O' MINGAIN Mongan O' Mongain Mingain	18	(26)
MITCHELL O' Mulvihil Milvihil See Mulville	82 Norman	
MOGNE O' Medog Maddhog Ma Otdog	75	(32)
de MOLEYNS See O' Devlin	77-115	
O'MOLINA O' Maoilfhiona	70	(14)
O' MOLLANE O' Melain O' Maolain	92	(6)
MOLLOY O' Maolmhuaidh	90	
MONAHAN O' Mhuineachain O' Muineacain See O' Meehan	39-97	
MONDY See Mac Gloin		
MONGAN See O' Mingain	18	(18-29)
MONK Mac an Mhanaigh O' Manachain O' Monaghan Mac Evanny See O' Manahan	39	(7-15-22)

MONTAGUE
See Tigue

MONTGOMERY   102   (22)
Mac Iomair
Mac Iver   Norse
Mac Geever

MOON   71
O' Mochain   (13-14-19)
Moghan
Mochane
Mahon

MOONEY   92
O' Maonaigh   (1-13-20)
Meeny of Sligo
Mainey of Munster

O' MOORA   43
 of Craobh

O' MOORE   38-40   (24)
O' Mordha
O' More

O'MOORE   43   (24)
 of Leix
O' Morna

MORAN   41-73
O' Mhuirein   (14-15-18-19)
Murran

O' MORANN   53
O' Mughroin

O' MORCHOE   94   (32)
O' Murchadha
Branch of Murphy

MORGAN   92   (16)
O' Muireagain
O' Murrigin
Merrigan
Murrican

MORIARTY   17   (26)
O' Muircheartaigh

O' MORNA   69

MAC MORRIN   53-60-94 (7)
Mac Moruinn
Mac Morrough

MAC MORROUGH   94
See Mac Morrin

MORTIMER   112
Mac Murty   Norman-English

MOYNIHAN   92   (26-27)
O' Muimhneachain
O' Mionagain
O' Minchain
Minahane

O' MULCONRY   76   (7)
O' Maolchonaire
Mulchrone

O' MULDERRY   89   (2)
O' Maoldoraidh

MULDOON   73-91   (7)

O' MULFOVER   73
O'Maelfoghmhair

MULKIERAN   92   (1-7-19)
O' Maolchiarain
O' Maoilciarian
O' Mulchiarin

MULLAN   80-81   (3-4)
O' Mellan
See O' Mullen

O'MULLEN   18-91
Mac Mullen   (2-3-4-23)
See Mullan

MULLIGAN   88
O' Maolagain   (1-8-14)
Mulqueen
Baldwin
Diamond

MULLINEAUX   82-115 (18)
Molineaux   Norman
Mullineux

MULLOY
See Molloy

MULQUEEN   98
O' Maolchaoin   (14-22-30)
O' Mulkeen

MULRENNAN   57   (7-15)

MULROONEY O' Maolruanaid See Rooney	25	(7)

O' MURLEY 24
O' hUrthoile (22-27-30)
See O' Hurly

MULVILLE 82 (22-26)
O' Maoilmhichil
O' Mulvihill Norman
O' Milvihil
Mitchell

MURPHY 94
O' Murchadha (7-18-27-32)

MAC MURRAY 56 (7-10)
Mac Muireadhaigh
O' Murray
Gilmore
Branch of O' Ruarc

O' MUNCHAIN 17

MURCHISON 82 (4)
Mac Murchaidh
O' Murcha Scotch
Murchie

MURRONY 25 (22)
O' Moroney
O' Maolrunanaidh
See Rooney

MAC MURDC 28

MAC MURROUGH 94 (32)
Mac Murchadha
Kavanagh
Kinsella
Hendrick
Mernagh

MURDOCK 32 (1-22)
Mac Muircheartaigh
Mac Murtrie
Mac Brearty

n

MAC NAGHTIN 69 (1)
Mac Naught
Mac Knight

MAC NEELY 48 (19)
Mac Conneelly
Mac Congaile
Connolly
Kennelly

MAC NAMARA 98 (22)
Mac Conmara

NEENAN 97 (22)
Naoindionain

MACNAMEE 87 (15)
Mac Conailloie
Mac Connellogues
Mac Namanamee

NEICE 40 (4-8)
Neeson
Mac Nadis

NAUGHTON 53-98
O' Neachtann (15-19-22)
Norton
O' Quinn

O' NEILL 24-78 (4-22)

O' NENY 69-73 (8-22)

O' NEACHACH 43

MAC NERLIN 88 (1-13)
Mac an Fhirleighinn
Mac Killerean

NEARNEY
See Mac Iniry

O' NECHTAN 53 (15-19)
See Naughton

NERNY 25
See Mac Inerney

NEEDHAM 13 (23)
See Neville

NESSON   40   (8)
Mac Aonghusa
Mac Neece
Branch of Mac Guinness

NESTOR   42   (22)
Mac an Adhastair
Mac an Agastair
Mac Nestor
Branch of O' Loughlin
  of Burren

NEVILLE   13   (23)
O' Neidhe

O'NEYLAND   71   (22)
O' Niallain
O' Neill of Bunrutty

MAC NICHOL   14   (2-3)

NICHOLLS   97   (3)
O' Niachol
Nicholson

MAC NICHOLS   112   Ulster
See Nixon

MAC NIE   13
Mac Niana

O' NEILLAN   69
of Armagh

NIXON   112
Mac Nicholls   (3-7-11)
Mac Nioclair
Mac Niclais
Clausson

NOGENT   59   (15)
Branch of O' Conor
  of Connacht

O'NOLAN   29-50
O' Nullain   (15-19-21-31-32)
O' Nunan
Knowlan
Noland
See Holohan

NORTON   53-98
O' Neachtann   (15-18-19-22)
Mac Naghtin
Naughton

NOTT   115
Norman

MAC NULTY   75   (1-4)
Mac an Ultaigh
See Mac Anulty and
  Mac Awley

O

MAC OGHIE   19
Oghy
See Mac Eochadh

OGILVY   59
Ogilby   Scotch
See O' Gilbey

OSIAN   97   (14-19)
O' hOisin

OWENS   20-24-56
O' Eoghain   (10-13-15-18-27)
Mac Keown   Welsh
See Hinds

p

MAC PADDEN   115   (14)
Mac Phaidin   Norman
Mac Evilly
See Barrett

MAC PATRICK   Norman
See de Courcy

PATTERSON	115	(17)
Paidin		
Padine	Norman	
Branch of Barrett		

PAYTON	76	(1)
O'Peatain		
Peyton	English	
Pattan		

PERKINS
See O' Fercinn

PETTY	115	(17-26)
Peitid		
Petit	Norman	

O' PHELAIN	93	(28-29)
O' Felain		
Ui Faelain		
O' Phelan		
O' Whelan		
See Mac Felan		

O'PHELAN	50	(29-32)
O' Faolain	Ulster	

MAC PHILBIN	112	(14-19)
Philbin		
Branch of Burke	Norman	

POWER	115	(28)
le Poer		

PLUNKETT	25-115
O' Pluingceid	Norman

PENDERGAST	115	(14)
de Priondragas		
See Mac Maurice		

PRICE	107
ap Rhys	Welsh

q

MAC QUEEN	79	(1)
See Mac Sweeney	Scotch	

QUILEY	98	(1-2)
O' Coigligh		

QUILLAN	21
Quillen	
See Collins	

MAC QUILLAN	115	(3)
Mac Uighilin		
Mac Cullen	Norman-Welsh	
Mac Llewelyn		
Branch of Mandeville		

QUILLIGAN
See Culligan

O' QUIN	76-79-98	
O' Chuinn	(3-4-16-22)	
O' Coine		
Coyne		
O' Quinn		

QUINCY	115
de Quiney	Norman

O' QUINLAN	75	(23-26)
O' Coindealbhain		
O' Coinleain		
Conlan		
Connellan		
Kindellan		

R

RANALD	41	(16)
Conmaicne		

MAC RANNALL	102	(30)
Mac Raghnaill	Norse	
Reynolds		

158

MAC RAYMOND 112 (26-27)
of Kerry Norman
See Redmond

O' READY 24 (18-29)
Mac Cready
Ready
Reddy

O' REALLY 55 (11-12)
O' Raghailligh
See O' Reilly

REARDEN 32 (27)
O' Rioghbhardain
O' Raiardan

O'REDDIE 41 (29)
O' Roidigh
Ruddy
See O' Roddy

REDICAN 41 (14)
O' Roideachain
O' Redahan
Reddican

REDMOND 94 (32)
of Wexford
Branch of Mac Murrough

MAC REDMOND 112 (19-20)
Mac Reamoinn Norman
Branch of Burke

O'REGAN 25-92
O' Riagain (14-15-22-24-27)
O' Ragan

REGINALD 14
See Mac Rannall

O' REILLY 55 (11)
O' Raghailligh

REYNOLDS 14-41
Mag Ragnaill (3-9-10-18)
Mac Randall
Reginald Norman
Olis

RICE 107
ap Rhyes (3-5-9-18)

MAC RICHARD 81-113 (32)
Rickard

de RIDELSFORD 115
Norman

RIDER 29 (22)
O' Marcachain
Ryder

RING 17 (27)
O' Billrin

O'RIORDAN 19-32
O' Rioghbhardain (26-27-30)
Reardan

ROCHE 115
de Rupe Norman

O' RODY 41 (19)
O' Rodaig
Reddie
Roddy

ROGERS 65 (2)
Mac Ruaidhri English
Rodgers
Mac Rory

ROONEY 25 -34-58
O' Runaighean (1-6-13)
of Sligo
O' Ruanaidh
of Down
O' Rooneen
of Donegal

O'ROURKE 55 (10)
O' Ruairc

MAC RUDDERY 115 (17)
Mac an Ridire Norman
Mac Knight
Branch of Fitzsimmons

RUTLEDGE 57 (1-4)
O' Maoiloicheirge
O' Maoildeirg
Reddington

RYAN 94
O' Maoilriain (10-18-19-
Mulrine 23-30)
Mulroyne
O' Mulryan

O' RYAN   25 (14-15)
O' Raigan

S

SAINT JOHN   115 (23-32)
See O' Singin   Norman

de SALISBURY   115
                       Norman

O'SCANLIN   43-72
O' Scannlain   (7-13-27)
O' Scannell
 of Sligo
O' Scanlon

SCULLY   98   (17)
O' Scolaidhe

SEGRU   18   (26)
O' Siochfhradha
O' Shighrowe   Norse
O'Siocfrada
O' Siocrada
Sugrve
Branch of O' Sullivan Mor

O'SEIGHAN   95
 of Kilshine

MAC SEOININ   112
Jennings   Norman
Branch of Burke

SEXTON   24
O' Seasnain   (11-27-30)

O' SHANAHAN   25
O' Siodhachain   (23-26-27-32)
O' Seanachain
O' Seanain
Shannon
Sheen
O' Sheehan

SHANE   41   (26)
 of Westmeath
Branch of O' Farrell

MAC SHANE   80   (9)
Mac Seain
Branch of O' Neill

SHANLEY   41   (10)
Mag Seanlaoic
Mac Seanloich
Ganley
Gantley
Shanlie

SHANNON
See O' Shanahan

O' SHAUGHNESSY   72   (19-30)
O' Seachnasaigh

O' SHEE   47   (26-27)
O' Shaghdha
O' Shea

MAC SHEEDY   98   (22)

O' SHEEHAN   25   (26-27)
O' Siodhachain
O' Sheahan

MAC SHEEHY   65
Mac Sithigh   (8-26-30)
O' Sheeky
 of Monagahan   Scotch
Mac Sheekie
Branch of Mac Donald
 of Limerick

MACK SHEEKIE   65   (30)
Mac Sheehy
Mac Sithigh
See Mac Sheehy

SHEEN
See O' Shanahan

SHERA   97
Mac Seartha
Branch of Fitzpatrick

MAC SHERRY   115 (27)
Hodnet   Norman

SHIEBY 73 (19)
O' Seibhleain
Branch of O' Shaughnessy

SHIELDS 82
O' Siadhail (1-3-6-20)
O' Siadail
O' Sheil

MAC SHONEEN 115
O' Keoneen Norman

O' SINGIN 93 (23)
Suingean Norman

MAC SIODA 98 (22)
Mac Sheedy
Branch of Mac Namara

SLATTERY 24 (22)
O' Slatraigh
O' Slatara

SMITH 43-115
of Down (6-10-22)
Mac an Ghabhann
O' Gabhann
of Sligo Norman-English
O' Gowan
of Cavin
Mac Gowan
See Mac an Gainiov

SOMERS 54-57
O' Somachain (13-18-32)
of Sligo
Mac Shamhradhain
Summers
Branch of Mac Govern
of Ulster
See Horican

MAC SPARRAN 66 (2-3)
Mac an Sparain

SPELLMAN 25 (15-19)
See Spelman

SPELMAN 25 (26-27)
O' Spelain
O' Spillane

STANTON 115
See Mac Aveely Norman

STAUNTON 115 (14)
de Stonndun

STEELE 65 (2-3)

STEWART 68 (7)
Mac Amhlaoibh
Mac Aulay
Branch of Maguire

STRONG BOW 114
(Ritchard Fitzgilbert)

MAC SWEENY 62-79
Mac Suibhne (1-5-26-27)

MAC SWINE 101 (1)
Mac Swiney

O'SULLIVAN 18 (26-27)
O' Suilleban

SUMMERS
See Somers

t

TANGNEY 21 (12)
O' Teangana
Branch of Mac Elligott

TARTAR 65 (3)
Ui Tuirtre
Turtyre

MAC TERNAN 55-67 (9-10)
Mac Tighearnain
Mac Tiernan

THACHAIR 97
Togher

MAC THEOBALD 82
Norman

MAC THOMAS	110	(18)
Mac Thomaisin		
Branch of Fitzgerald		

THORNTON 21 (30)
See O' Meehan English

O'TIERNY 43
O' Tighearnaigh (1-14-17)

TIGUE 68 (19)
Mac Taidhg
Branch of O' Kelly

TILLY 93 (7-16)
O' Tathligh
O' Tily
Mac Tully
Mac Atilla

TIMMONS 115 (14)
Mac Toimin
Thomas
Branch of Barrett

O'TOGHILL 93 (2)
O' Tuathail
Branch of O' Toole

TOLAND 93 (14)
O' Tuathalain
Branch of O' Toole

TONER 76 (1-2-3)
O' Tomnair

O' TOOLE 53-93
O' Tuathail (14-21-25)

O' TORMEY 25 (11-17)
O' Tormada
Tarmey

TRACY 17-76-82-92
O' Treasaigh (7-23-24)
O' Tracey

O'TRAVER 13
de Traibears (18-25-27)
Travor Norman

TUCKER 75 (19-22)
O' Tougher
O' Tuachair
O' Tuathchair

TULLY 93
Ui Mael Tuile (19-18-22)
Flood

MAC TUMELTY 24
Mac Tomaltaigh (6-9-15)

O' TUOMY 25 (27-30)
of Limerick
Toomey
Towmey
O' Tuama

O'TURNEY 41 (26-27)
O' Tonry
O' Torna
O' Turny
O' Dorney
of Cork

TYRRELL 115 (17)
de Tirial Norman

O' TYNE 41 (22)
O' Teimhin
O' Thynne
O' Tyn

U

UARGHUSA 97

UGGIN 77
Higgins (3-4-18)
O' hUigin
See O' Hagan

O' UICA 93

162

U

| VERDON | 115 | (9) |
de Bheardun
de Verdon   Norman

MAC VICKERS   69   (2-3)
Mac an Bhiocaire   Scotch
Branch of Mac Mahons

W

WALDRON   114
Mac an Bhaildrun (14-15-18)
Branch of   Norman
 Costello

WALSH   115
Breathnach   (14-18-19-30)
                 Norman

MAC WALTER   112
Mac Ualtair   Norman

MAC WARD   43   (1-19)
Mac an Bhaird

WELLESLEY   110
Mac Bhaldraithe
Wesley

O' WESTROPP   18   (22-30)
Branch of   English-Irish
 O'Calligan

WHELAN   50   (23-32)
O' Faolain
Hyland
Branch of O' Phelan

WHITE   98   (11)
 of Cavin
de Faoit

MAC WILLIAM   112 (2-3)
Mac Uilliam   Scotch-Norman

WILLIAMS   112
               (3-18-27)
                 Norman

WOLF   98   (30)
de Bhulbh   Norman

BIBLIOGRAPHY

THE VIKINGS
Johannes Brondsted
Penguin Books   1970
Harmondsworth and London

CELTIC MYTHOLOGY
Proinsias Mac Cana
The Hamlyn Publishing Group
London   1970

A TREASURY OF IRISH FOLKLORE
Padraic Colum
Crown Publishing Company
New York   1967

A VIEW OF THE IRISH LANGUAGE
Brian O'Cuiv
The Stationary Office
Dublin   1969

MANUSCRIPT MATERIALS OF
 IRISH HISTORY
Eugene O'Curry

MYTHS AND FOLKLORE OF IRELAND
Jeremiah Curtin   1890
Republished, Weathervane Books
New York

IRISH - ENGLISH DICTIONARY
Rev. Patrick S. Dinneen MA
The Educational Co. of Ireland
Dublin, 1927, Reprint 1970

ANNALA RIOGHACTA EIREANN
(The Annals of the Kingdom
 of Ireland)
By the four masters
Translation, John O'Donovan
Hodges, Smith and Company
Dublin   1854

CONOR CRUISE O'BRIEN
 INTRODUCES IRELAND
Editor Owen D. Edwards
McGraw-Hill Book Company
New York   1968

IRISH FOLK WAYS
E. Estyn Evans
Routledge & Kegan Paul Ltd.
London   1957

AMERICA B.C.
Barry Fell
Quadrangle-New York Times
Book Company   1976

ENCYCLOPAEDIA OF IRELAND
Allen Figgis & Co. Ltd.
Dublin   1968

THE GERALDINES
Brian Fitzgerald
Devin-Adair Company
New York   1952

THE ANNALS OF CONNACHT
Editor, A. Martin Freeman
Dublin Institute of Advanced
 Studies
Dublin   1944

PADDY THE COPE
Patrick Gallagher
Devin-Adair Co.
Old Greenwich, Conn.   1942

A HISTORY OF IRELAND
Mac Geoghan

GUIDE TO NATIONAL MONUMENTS
 OF IRELAND
Peter Harbison
Gill & MacMillan
Dublin   1970

ANNALS OF LOUGH CE'
Editor, W. M. Hennessy

Dublin   1939

ANNALS OF ULSTER
Editors, W. M. Hennessy and
 B. Mac Carthy

Dublin   1887

ANNALS OF ULSTER
Editors, W. M. Hennessy and
 B. Mac Carthy

Dublin   1887

IRISH PEDIGREES, THE
 ORIGINAND STEM OF
 THE IRISH NATION
John O'Hart
1892 - 1976
The Genealogical Publishing
 Company, Baltimore

EUROPAS FYRSTESLAEGTER
En Genealogisk Nogle
Robert W. Harvest and
 Helga Tulinius
Politikens Forlag   1977

A LITERARY HISTORY OF
 IRELAND FROM EARLIEST
 TIMES TO THE PRESENT DAY
Douglas Hyde, LLD

SOCIAL HISTORY OF
 ANCIENT IRELAND
P. W. Joyce

HISTORY OF THE NATIONS, IRELAND
Patrick W. Joyce LLD
P. F. Collier & Son
New York   1928

THE IRISH MYTHOLOGICAL CYCLE
D'Arbois de Jubainville
Hodges and Figgis
Dublin   1903

FORAS FEASA ar EIRINN
(The History of Ireland)
Geoffrey Keating
London   1902

DEAR DARK HEAD
Helen Landreth
Whittlesey House
McGraw-Hill Book Company
New York   1936

IRISH FAMILIES
Edward MacLysaght D.Litt
Crown Publishers
New York   1972

SURNAMES OF IRELAND
Edward MacLysaght
Irish University Press
Dublin   1973

THE STORY OF THE IRISH RACE
Seumas Mac Manus
Devin-Adair Company
New York and Old Greenwich
 Conn.

ANNALS OF CLONMACNOISE
Translation, C. Mageoghagan
Editor, Rev. Denis Murphy S.J.
The University Press
Dublin   1896

PHASES OF IRISH HISTORY
Eoin Macneill
Gill and Son
Dublin   1968

CENSUS OF IRELAND 1659
Editor, Seamus Pender
Dublin   1939

THE ROYAL HORDES
E. D. Phillips
Thames and Hudson
London   1965

THE DRUIDS
Stuart Piggott
Penguin Books
Harmondsworth and London   1974

THE VIKING SETTLEMENTS OF
 NORTH AMERICA
Frederick J. Pohl
Clarkson N. Potter, Inc.
New York   1972

THE CELTS
Georges Dutton
Translation, David MacRae
Minerva S.A.
Geneva   1977